Success Strategies

Published by Insight Publishing
647 Wall Street • Sevierville, Tennessee • 37862

10 9 8 7 6 5 4 3 2

DISCLAIMER: This book is a compilation of ideas from numerous experts who have each contributed a chapter. As such, the views expressed in each chapter are of those who were interviewed and not necessarily of the interviewer or Insight Publishing.

PRINTED IN THE UNITED STATES OF AMERICA

ISBN-13: 978-1-60013-219-3
ISBN-10: 1-60013-219-7

Table of Contents

A Message from the Publisher...

Strategic planning is vital to achieving success in any endeavor in life. Whether you are an entrepreneur, a corporate CEO, a volunteer for a community project, or trying to organize your personal life, it's important to have strategies in place that will help you succeed.

I am really excited about what the authors in this book had to say. If I had not interviewed these outstanding, successful men and women I don't think the subjects they talked about would have occurred to me. Who would have thought "reinventing diversity" or "the power of procrastination" would be success strategies?

One of the authors in this chapter said that we are performing in an era where knowledge is power. He went on to say, "I think the key is applying that knowledge with laser-like focus. This means ruthless prioritization on what needs to be accomplished in order to yield the highest payoff in cultures of high-demand."

The chapters in this book will help you discover core issues that may be challenging you or keeping success just out of reach. I am sure that you will be able to use the information these authors have shared to empower your dreams and goals into reality.

Remember, success doesn't just happen—*you make it happen.*

Interviews conducted by:
David E. Wright
President, International Speakers Network

Chapter One

An interview with...

Howard Ross

Reinventing Diversity

David Wright (Wright)

Today we're talking with Howard Ross, founder and Chief Learning Officer of Cook Ross, Inc. He is considered one of the country's thought leaders on leading organizational change, diversity, and cultural competency. Howard has worked with hundreds of organizations both in and out of the United States over the past twenty-five years including large corporations, healthcare providers, non-profits, governmental organizations, and the media. Howard serves as a trusted coach and confidant to numerous CEOs and executive teams. In perhaps one of Cook Ross' most high-profile interventions, Howard worked with the Atlanta Braves after the infamous John Rocker incident. Cook Ross, Inc. specializes in helping organizations develop cultures that are more inclusive, more culturally competent, and more able to maximize their productivity and profitability through effective diversity management. Howard was chosen by the Johnetta B. Cole Diversity Institute to be the 2007–2008 Visiting Professor of Diversity at Bennett College for Women, a Historically Black Women's College in Greensboro, North Carolina. He is the first white man to receive this honor.

Howard, welcome to *Success Strategies!*

Howard Ross (Ross)

Thank you, David; it's good to be with you.

Wright

The word "diversity" has been around for quite some time and has been interpreted in many different ways. You refer to "diversity," "inclusion," and "cultural competency" in your work. How would you define these terms?

Ross

I think that when we look at the history of the diversity conversation, it's evolved over the years. When we look back at organizations forty or more years ago, the real issue was that we had an overwhelmingly large number of white men dominating the environment. As late as 1965, which was only two generations ago, 64 percent of the American workforce was made up of native-born white men. So in those times a particular paradigm was created in which white men were clearly the dominant group and others were somewhat monolithically called women and minorities.

Women and "people of color" of those days were the non-dominant group. Inside of that paradigm we saw one group holding the reigns, generally either being ignorant of the dynamics that were going on or overtly biased, and the other group being interested in justice and fairness and having opportunity, trying to get into organizations in positions of opportunity with the predominant group resisting that and basically working toward preserving the status quo. It looked "normal."

In those days the diversity conversation emerged and it was predominantly about getting people into organizations and being sure they were treated fairly once they were there. Now we know that in many situations that's still the case, but we also know that it's evolved to the point where now, after we look at the environment that we have today, native-born, heterosexual white men make up between 42 and 48 percent of the environment. When we include other people that we might consider non-dominant groups, such as gays and lesbians, bisexuals, and people who are immigrants from other countries but also white-skinned, we're probably more to the low end of that—the 42 percent.

In this scenario we now have a tremendously multi-cultural work environment. We have people from many, many different racial groups, ethnic groups, cultural groups, religious groups, as well as some of the other areas of diversity.

So getting people in the work force is not our only issue right now; in the current scenario it's important for people to be included so that they have opportunities in leadership and engagement and decision-making—that's where the whole inclusion part of it comes from. We may have people already there, but we want to make sure they are fully integrated, fully engaged, and fully empowered.

The third aspect, and what we think is the most advanced form of understanding relative to these issues, is what we refer to as cultural competency or cultural flexibility.

By cultural competency what we are referring to are organizations that have developed the skills and resources and the systems and structures to understand and be able to respond to the vast differences of people who come from different cultural and ethnic groups, etc. In addition, we need individuals who have developed the flexibility to modify their behavior, when appropriate, to meet the cultural patterns of others who may have come from different backgrounds.

For example, in health care today, we know that there are doctors and nurses who have to respond to patients who come from sometimes as many as a hundred different countries, and often with needs that are tremendously different. These needs are not only what we might consider some of the "soft" areas (communication, family patterns, etc.), but also things like genetic polymorphisms that could affect the way drugs impact one group versus another. And so when we get to the stage where we're really beginning to include culture and difference in the way that we anticipate how we are going to interact with and treat people, then we're beginning to get culturally competent and culturally flexible.

Wright

What do you think are some of the main reasons that diversity efforts so often fail to produce the results that are hoped for?

Ross

Whenever we get into paradigm thinking, we know that paradigms can be tremendously expansive and they can be tremendously limiting. The paradigms relative to diversity can go off in different directions, but there are some that generally have limited action in the way we look at things.

The assumption often is that diversity is really just about equal employment opportunity (EEO) and affirmative action. So when people hear "diversity" sometimes what they think is that it is just being sure they don't get sued or making sure they get people into the environment. And of course, both of those things are important, but they are just a very small part of the diversity conversation.

The second is that diversity is often seen is as just a race or a gender issue. This is a belief that is very prevalent and not surprising given that a lot of the challenge and the negative energy we've experienced about diversity has come from these distinctions. Nonetheless these are sometimes seen as the "only" areas of focus. We now know that there are many other significant areas: religion, disabilities, and sexual orientation. Age is a major factor right now in the American workplace environment. Things like personality, politics, and work styles, are all factors as well.

The third paradigm that is limiting sometimes is that diversity is seen as just a touchy-feely human resources issue—it's not the "real business." Of course we now know that this concept is really passé as we begin to see more and more businesses reorienting to all of the different ways that diversity impacts them. They are now focusing on the demographics of their work force and the demographics of their market share, recruitment issues, and retention issues. They are asking questions such as: How are we going to keep the best people once we get them? How are we going to get these young talented people to come to *our* organization rather than another one? Then, of course, there is the whole issue of legal liability as well as how we develop business. How do we develop business when our clients are looking for more diversity?

In addition to all of that, we now know that the kind of environments we have and how creative and productive we are, are all impacted by diversity. Robert Putnam, who wrote the landmark book *Bowling Alone*, in 2000 recently revealed the results of a study he conducted. He spoke to 30,000 people in diverse communities around the country and found that this diversity, when not properly managed, results in what he refers to as a "turtling" effect—people retreat into their natural similar groups rather than truly integrating.

On the other hand, there's a wonderful new book by a University of Michigan professor named Scott Page titled *The Difference.* Using mathematical formulations, Page studies the impact of diversity on creativity and productivity and proves categorically that it has a positive impact—when it is properly managed. The question then becomes, where are we going to end up on the Putnam-to-Page continuum? Are we going to manage it well and go the direction that Page identifies, or ignore it and end up where Putnam's research leads us?

The fourth paradigm is really a question: should we do diversity work simply because it's the right thing to do? Obviously a lot of us think it's the right thing to do, but many times people get stuck in that component as opposed to staying focused on the business, and therefore, when organizations run into a slow quarter they back off from it. There's also a tendency for diversity programs to be seen as getting people who have historically been outside of the "mainstream"—the folks in the groups we mentioned earlier—into the "mainstream" rather than looking at expanding the "mainstream" to include various different ways of doing things. And, of course, to do that we have to include everybody in the diversity conversation, including white men. Some of the cultures in our organizations were formed generations ago. It is time to re-evaluate what we need to create to be successful in this new world we're living in.

So those are just some of the reasons I think that people get stuck.

One last one is that often people see diversity as something that can be managed simply by sending people through training, and then it will be "fixed." But in order to create systemic and culture change in any area, you need to create a sustained plan for it and do it over time.

Wright

You often talk about the impact of "unconscious bias." What is unconscious bias and where does it come from?

Ross

In the framework of the conversation we've been having, one of the most pernicious paradigms of diversity has been the "good person/bad person" paradigm. This is the accepted notion. If people make decisions that differentially impact one group versus another they are doing it with negative intention and they are doing it with self-knowledge—that they actually know what they are doing. In reality, what we find now is that overwhelming evidence shows that most of the decisions people make impacting one group negatively relative to another are made without their even realizing they are making them. For example, Malcolm Gladwell, in his book *Blink,* mentions a couple of examples of this lesson: 15 percent of American men are over six feet tall, yet over 60 percent of corporate CEOs are over six feet tall; less than 4 percent of American men are over six feet two inches, and yet 36 percent of corporate CEOs are over six feet two inches. Now I'd guess, having worked with a lot of corporate boards of directors in my career, that very few boards set out to find a tall guy to lead their organizations and yet this happens quite unconsciously because of the bias people tend to have toward tall people as leaders relative to short people. We find much evidence now that indicates the same thing is true relative to age, gender, and relative to many kinds of differences. Body size is another example. We know that people who are overweight tend to get lower performance reviews compared with people who are physically fit. We know that in classroom environments, boys who raise their hands are often called on more frequently than girls who raise their hands. We now realize that most of these things are happening unconsciously.

This changes the way we approach diversity quite dramatically. First, because it means we have to be more vigilant to be sure to understand the "unseen" as well as the obvious. Second, when we address the issue of diversity, we encounter and even encourage resistance because a person's response is, "Well, I didn't do that on purpose! I didn't mean anything by that." They become defensive, whether or not their motives were intentional or unintentional. Whereas, if we can begin to understand the bias is actually a very normal human function—it's something that we all do—we can stop and look inwardly and understand it in ourselves. We'd do a better job of interacting with people and reaching them.

So we've begun working with some folks now at some of the major universities who are studying this including Harvard University, the University of Washington, and the University of Virginia. These universities have a three-university consortium called Project Implicit to study this. We are examining the research they've developed to uncover some of these unconscious patterns and find ways that the research findings can be used to help people to see these habits in themselves so they can change their behavior with others.

Wright

Why is it that people see things so differently from each other?

Ross

We are born into different cultural narratives, you might say "the stories of our lives," and we are impacted in different ways by them. We're not born into a particular belief system or identity when we're born.

About four years ago my oldest two twin grandchildren were born and I was in the hospital the next day holding them in my hands. I looked down at them and it occurred to me that they didn't know they were girls rather than boys, they didn't know that they were bi-racial (their mom is Indian), and they didn't know that they came from two different religious traditions (we call them Hind-Jews). All of that was invisible to them!

Over time, of course, all of these different factors and experiences would impact the way they saw the world. This happens in a number of ways. On one level we learn things from our culture. We learn certain patterns that are pretty obvious—the ways we dress and the things we eat and the way we celebrate holidays and all those kinds of things. But we also learn more subtle things like patterns of communication and eye contact.

You mentioned in the introduction that I'd worked with the Atlanta Braves. When I was working with them, one of the players on the team was from Venezuela. He told me a wonderful story that is an example of culture in action. He was raised in a culture in which young men were taught that the way you show respect for an adult authority figure is by averting your eyes when you're speaking to them. Then he was signed as a seventeen-year-old and sent to his first minor league team.

On the first day the manager came over to talk to him. The young recruit did what he was taught to do his whole life—very politely he averted his eyes. The manager then started yelling at him, "Damn it! Look at me when I'm talking to you!"

The player told me, "I looked up at him, but I could feel my father's hand about to slap me all the way from Venezuela!"

So culture shows up in all of these subtle ways. Value systems can be quite different depending upon the influences of various parts of the world that we come from. The things that we find important, our axiologies or value systems, the way that we prioritize, the heuristics that we use (i.e., the way we solve problems), our perceptions, our interpretations of things, our language, all of these things are affected by culture. That's one major area that impacts the way we see things.

The second area is the understanding of our own group identity. What I mean by that is we see ourselves in a particular way in context not only by what happens to us but also what's happened to people like us. So if a person grows up as an African-American in the United States, they see themselves in the context of the history of African-Americans in the United States, which includes of course slavery and discrimination, etc. All of that affects them in the same way that Jews are affected by our past history or women are affected by their past history or, for that matter, white men or immigrants or people from any other cultural group. Each of us has an experience in ourselves based on what we've seen and what we've noticed.

A young child walks into his or her elementary school and sees the forty-three pictures of the presidents of the United States on the wall. If the child is a young, white, Christian boy, when he sees the presidents he will see the message is that you can be anything you want in life as long as you work hard enough and are smart enough and keep going for it. If the child is a young girl or a child of color or somebody of a different religion, what he or she sees is, "Not me, not me, not me." The message is quite different. The message is that no matter how hard you work in life or how smart you are, there are certain limitations to how far you can go.

All of those influences also play a role in our development of identity.

The third area is the individual experiences we've had. We are treated a particular way because we're a part of a particular group or we have personal experiences that affect us.

And the last piece is that over the course of our lives we find ourselves in various circumstances, in groups and organizations we are a part of, and places we become affiliated with over time. In our affiliation with those groups, we begin to embody some of their values. This can affect somebody who, for example, spends time in the military in the way he or she looks at the world and the behaviors he or she chooses, the way the person acts, and the way he or she operates. The same thing is true for moving into a particular city or even working in a particular company.

So all of this begins to create a sense of identity or contributes to creating our sense of identity. I call it our "perceptual lens." And while we were born with no real sense of identity, what Carl Jung, the famous Swiss psychologist used to refer to as the "dis-identified self," over time this evaporates and we become a particular way because of all these things we've learned. These things have given us a particular lens through which we see the world. It impacts everything: how we act, what our world view is, our attitudes and emotions, the way we identify ourselves, and things that are important to us. It also impacts the sense of self-image we have, which can be affected by this as well. We have known this for years.

Probably the most famous example of this impact on self-image and the way it contributes to internalized negative self-images is the famous study that Kenneth Clark did with the white and black dolls experiment involving young children that contributed to the Brown vs. Board of Education decision. It's important to recognize that it also can create a sense of entitlement. If I grow up as a member of a dominant group, I often have a stronger sense that people are interested in me. I can say what I want to say. If I were a member of a non-dominant group, I might be more hesitant and not sure about expressing myself fully.

All of those factors contribute to the lens through which we see the world.

Wright

How do you help people address issues of unconscious bias?

Ross

One of the things that we try to do, and we find this critically important, is to create a safe container for people to engage in dialogue about these issues. I don't mean that to sound like jargon. What I mean is, how do we create an environment in which people can feel comfortable really exploring their own issues? If, as I said earlier, people feel that having a negative attitude toward one group versus another makes them a bad person, most people will be defensive and not want to engage. If we can create an environment where people realize that this is a human phenomenon and that all human beings do it—that they are not a bad person for doing it—then we can begin to really explore and change behaviors if necessary.

So the first thing is to create a safe environment for people to engage in the dialog. Once we've done that, then using some of the distinctions we've been talking about, we invite people to begin to explore themselves and understand their cultural narrative: "Where do my attitudes come from? Why do I believe that this is true? Is what I believe to be true really true, or is it just a strongly held point of view on my part? Is it something that I believe is true just because of the way I've been raised and the things I've learned, etc.? And if that's the case, do I want to continue to operate from that belief system, or do I want to open up to the possibility that there are other belief systems that might better serve me and the people I interact with? Am I willing to talk openly with people from other groups to learn a little bit more about them so that I can balance my (perhaps) biased belief systems with rationality and reason and understanding what's really there?" So information is another piece of that.

Transformation, education, information are all critical pieces to transform the way people look at themselves. Loosening up some of the rigidity about "the way things are," educating ourselves to understand more of what is going on around us, and then informing ourselves of both our internal process and the way we interact with others will help make us culturally competent.

Wright

How has globalization impacted the need for understanding diversity and becoming culturally competent?

Ross

It's actually critical because we know now the trend of business is toward globalization. We are dealing with companies all the time that work outside of the United States or sell their product outside of the United States.

I heard somebody from Colgate Palmolive for example, recently say that 76 percent of their product is sold outside of the United States. So we know that if American companies are going to be positioning themselves to work outside of this country, we have to understand at a deeper level than ever before the cultural patterns of other countries. We also need to understand the way that potential market share and those people who are going to be working for us there interact and the way that they see the world.

In addition to that, we know that there's more movement of people in and out of the United States than ever before. The rate of immigration has increased dramatically and we are going through the most robust period of immigration in our nation's history. A lot of people don't realize this, but more than 50 percent of the people who are living in the United States today who were born outside of this country, have come to this country since 1990. The number of foreign-born residents, by the way, is almost 12 percent—the highest since the nineteenth century. In addition, whereas in the past an overwhelming number of these immigrants were white Europeans, today they are from South and Central America, Africa, Asia, the Caribbean, and the Middle East.

These are places where people don't only look different, but their cultural models may be more different than what we have known as "mainstream" American culture. In addition, people are maintaining their cultural identities and languages more than ever before.

So we are talking about a dramatic impact created by people who are working in our businesses, working in our organizations, and helping run municipal organizations. Globalization is not just a factor of "how do we market ourselves and position ourselves around the world in other countries," it's also recognizing that our country itself is becoming more globalized. In that context we have to break out of the rigidity in which we sometimes see our way of doing things as the only way, and begin to develop the cultural competency and cultural flexibility to move between different cultural values and different ways that we present ourselves. We must do this in a way that maintains our core operating values if we are going to maintain the integrity of our organizations.

Wright

What are some of the ways that you see the need for cultural competency occurring in the organizations you are working with?

Ross

It shows up in almost every way, but there are a couple of dramatic examples. The healthcare example we talked about earlier is one of them. We work with many hospitals and healthcare systems around the country; it's one of the larger segments of our business. We find some pretty extraordinary examples of cultures showing up as a distinction that impacts the quality of care. I want to be clear that I'm speaking in archetypes, not stereotypes. In other words, we can speak of archetypical patterns of behavior on the part of large groups of people and that doesn't mean that every person in that group acts that way. When we assume that they do, we are stereotyping them.

Archetypes can be helpful as a way of giving us distinctions to look at. Just one example: when Vietnamese women deliver babies in hospitals in the United States, they tend to become dehydrated more than other groups. The reason is not a biological one, it's a cultural one. Traditional Vietnamese cultural concepts of health are centered around the hot and cold theory. The archetypical pattern for Vietnamese women is they are told that childbirth is a "cold time." During cold times, they are told not to drink cold liquids or eat cold foods. But what does a nurse bring to a woman in labor? Ice chips and ice water! And so, Vietnamese women don't drink it. As a result they tend to get dehydrated. As a result of that they stay in the hospital longer, which affects hospitals financially. It can affect the mother's health, and it can impact lactation, therefore affecting the connection between the mother and the baby. All of this can be simply resolved by a nurse being aware of this and asking the woman, "What temperature would you like the water to be?"

In healthcare we are seeing a multiplicity of examples of diversity ranging from how we deal with patient needs to how we deal with family needs to what taboos about certain treatment modalities exist to how drugs impact different patients from different ethnicities because of genetic polymorphisms. In addition, we include diet, nutrition, and many other factors.

Lawyers deal with issues like reading the body language of potential jurors or witnesses on the witness stand. When we hire people and are managing them in different kinds of businesses, do we know what kind of feedback they like? How can we best communicate with them to encourage and inspire them? The same behavior that we think is inspirational to us may turn somebody else off. Do we understand communication patterns and how they are occurring? When we are teaching children in schools, do we understand that children who come from different cultural backgrounds may be used to different patterns of behavior, which might impact their learning in addition to the whole issue of language?

Those are just a few examples of the various ways that we are beginning to see the impact of cultural diversity.

Wright

How does one go about changing the culture of an organization to make it more inclusive and culturally competent?

Ross

We need to look at organizational culture development from a long-term standpoint, and not as something that is done on a dime. Changing a culture is like moving a battleship—it happens over time. One of the real breakdowns occurring in trying to change organizations' behavior is that people have thought it's pretty simple, and have the attitude that "we'll just send people through a training program and then they'll all change."

We realized that there's more than education and motivation involved. There's also the impact of normative structures of culture and understanding how we create a clear sense of what kinds of behavior are normal and abnormal. Most of us have gone to training programs where we encounter what I refer to sometimes as "the car wash phenomenon of training." People leave the training all excited and they're going to do all this new stuff; however, two weeks later the training materials are a dusty book on the shelf and the people are back to their old behavior.

So we start in a very systematic way—we start by trying to understand the culture. We sometimes do what we call an "organizational culture audit." This involves surveys or interviews or focus groups. We get a sense of how the culture is operating—what are the key leverage points that are making the culture operate the way it does? We look at everything ranging from how we recruit and hire people into the organization to how we orient them. We ask questions like: "What are the things they are most focused on once they are in the organization?" "How do we create the kind of structure in an organization that will support new kinds of behavior?" "What's the merit basis that people are evaluated on and given rewards for and held accountable to?" We look at all of these various factors. We also look at how the organization looks outside in the marketplace: What are the things that people see or believe about the organization? How does it represent itself? All of this information is gathered in a study. We will then generally sit down with a leadership team made up of a cross-functional group of people and create a goal and vision for the organization and a clear sense of direction about where to go and what to do.

One of the challenges we've had with diversity programs in the past is that most of them have been about fixing problems rather than creating a vision. Creating a vision is critically important because we know that human beings are most greatly inspired by having a vision in front of them. So we help people create a vision for what the organization will look like and how they will be behaving when they've achieved it. We then put in place the kind of activities that might include education efforts. They may be changing some systems and structures and they might be operating differently. It might involve team development work. There are all kinds of different things that help us get from Point A, which we discovered through our assessment, to Point B, the vision. The last stage is to have some kind of a process of accountability so that movement is being measured and fed back into the system so it becomes an on-going process.

One of the things we know about organizational culture is that they are always generating themselves. They either generate themselves by reaction to what is going on or we can pro-actively generate the kind of culture we want by focusing our attention on it.

Wright

What are the best ways to develop a diversity training initiative?

Ross

The first step is to go out and identify what's going on in your organization. There is no "one size fits all" and just because another organization has had success with a particular initiative doesn't mean it will work for you. Organizational cultures are unique, with distinctive issues, concerns, cultural norms, and histories. All of these factors contribute to what kind of training will work and the content and style of the training. I find that often people try to copy another organization's behavior and, frankly, sometimes we've contributed to that as consultants and trainers because we have a particular model that we use. When all you have is a hammer, everything looks like a nail to you, so the model becomes something we apply everywhere, rather than the needs of the organization driving the process.

I think it's important to understand what the specific needs are of the particular organization, and then find what some of the various approaches are that people are using to address those needs. Make sure that not only the approach but also the people you choose to work with are people who seem to fit with your organizational culture. The "right chemistry" is the language we use in personal relationships, but it's also applicable here because the people have to be a "good fit" to the organization. Then, once that's determined, the training should be customized so that it speaks the language of the organization in terms of examples, etc., that are relevant and that will get people internally involved.

Our favorite model for training is to combine an internal facilitator and trainer with one of our external folks over time, and then eventually to turn the training initiative over exclusively to internal people so they begin to develop the sustainability to be able to own it and have it be part of the organization's process rather than the consultant's work.

Wright

What do you think is the appropriate role for a diversity consultant?

Ross

The bottom line answer to that is to support the organization in moving forward and being independent of you as the consultant. It's like a good counselor—if we're really doing our job effectively, we're making ourselves obsolete. In many organizations, that happens over an extended period of time. In some organizations there's always a place where people might come back over time and check in with us for certain kinds of things; but I do think that our role is to bring in a broader sense of experience and exposure to the topic. We want to provide the organization with our ability to share best practices outside the organization. We want to be a mirror to the people within the organization, to be truth-tellers. Sometimes we have to "speak truth to power" and to say to people in leadership, "You may not be doing this intentionally, but your behavior is contributing to the problem." We want to let them know our best sense of what's really going on, and sometimes, as outsiders, we have the freedom and the responsibility to do or say what people on the inside would be on shaky ground doing/saying.

Again, it's especially important that we coach, develop, and train people internally to develop the expertise and the abilities—the knowledge, awareness, and skill—to be able to lead the process on their own. And then lastly, we should be available as an advisor, a coach, a supporter, even a friend for people to turn to when they are running into stumbling blocks so that we can help guide them along the path.

Wright

Given the increasingly diverse demographics of the workplace and the increase of globalization, what kinds of leaders will we need for organizations to thrive in the twenty-first century?

Ross

I think we've come back again to the conversation we started with about the shift in paradigms. I think most of us in organizations come from a background in which leaders were seen as supposedly being strong people and people who have the answers. Everybody falls in line and it's based upon the military model created back in the early twentieth century in business. In reality we know that the twenty-first century needs a different kind of leadership. People want to be more engaged—people want to be more involved with decisions that affect them. They want to have an opportunity to grow. Younger people especially are less patient and want to move faster than they ever did before.

The needs of the workforce are greater as well, relative to the differences we've been talking about in culture and perspective, etc. Twenty-first century leaders are going to have to be leaders who are culturally competent and culturally flexible. They have to be leaders who understand those differences. In order to be successful they have to be leaders who are less attached to having the answer, less attached to being the star who sells, and more committed to getting other people engaged, and more committed to learning.

Another factor in this is that we bring in young people today who have access to learning far beyond anything that people have ever had before. It used to be that if you were the boss, all you had to do was stay a half a step ahead of the people you were managing in any particular endeavor. Today, some of the younger people coming in have access to knowledge and information that gives them a greater capability in some cases than the people who are managing them.

Maintaining yourself as the smartest person and the one who can do it best doesn't necessarily make you the best leader. Sometimes what makes you the best leader is acknowledging that other people understand it better than you do, and giving others some rope to have a little bit more room to be creative and invent things—to teach you in conjunction with you being the one who's teaching.

Wright

This has been a great conversation. I've learned more about diversity here today than I've learned in the last fifty years! You sure know your subject. I've never even thought of some of these issues.

Ross

Thanks, David, I appreciate that!

About Howard Ross

HOWARD ROSS is the Founder and Chief Learning Officer of Cook Ross, Inc., one of the nation's leading organizational change, diversity, inclusion, and cultural competency consultancies. Ross has consulted with hundreds of organizations over more than twenty years of practice, including major corporations, healthcare providers, professional services firms, media, and governmental and community-based organizations. He coaches and works extensively with senior organizational leaders, and was honored to be chosen by President Julianne Malveaux, and the Johnetta B. Cole Institute as the 2007–2008 Visiting Professor of Diversity at Bennett College for Women.

Howard Ross
Cook Ross, Inc.
1515 Noyes Drive
Silver Spring, MD 20910
301.565.4035
howross@cookross.com
www.cookross.com

Chapter Two

An interview with . . .

Warren Bennis

Leadership Strategies

David Wright (Wright)

Today we are talking with Dr. Warren Bennis, Ph.D. He is a distinguished Professor of Business at the University of Southern California and Chairman of USC's Leadership Institute. He has written eighteen books including *On Becoming A Leader, Why Leaders Can't Lead,* and *The Unreality Industry,* coauthored with Ivan Mentoff. Dr. Bennis was successor to Douglas McGregor as Chairman of the Organizational Studies Department at MIT. He also taught at Harvard and Boston universities. Later he was Provost and Executive Vice President of the State University of New York at Buffalo and President of the University of Cincinnati. He has had over nine hundred articles published and two of his books have earned the coveted McKenzie Award for the "Best Book on Management." He has served in an advisory capacity for the past four U.S. presidents and as a consultant to many corporations and agencies, including the United Nations. Awarded eleven honorary degrees, Dr. Bennis has also received numerous awards including the Distinguished Service Award from the American Board of Professional Psychologists and the Perry L. Ruther Practice Award from the American Psychological Association.

Dr. Bennis, welcome to *Success Strategies.*

Dr. Warren Bennis (Bennis)

I'm glad to be here again with you, David.

Wright

In a conversation with *Behavior Online*, you stated that most organizations evaluate potential or emerging leaders by seven criteria: business literacy, people skills, conceptual abilities, track record, taste, judgment, and character. Because these terms were somewhat vague, you left them to be defined by the reader. Will you give our readers an unadorned definition of these criteria, as you define them?

Bennis

There's no precise dictionary definition that would satisfy me or maybe anyone. I'll just review them very quickly because there's a lot more we want to discuss.

Business literacy: do you know the territory, do you know the ecology of the business, do you know how it works, do you know where the plugs are, do you know who the main stakeholders are, and are you familiar with a thing called business culture?

People skills: This is your capacity to connect and engage because business leadership is about establishing, managing, creating, and engaging in relationships. Conceptual abilities are more important these days because they have to do with the paradoxes and complexities—the cartography—of stakeholders that make life at the top (more than ever) interesting and difficult, which is why we've had such a turnover in CEOs and leaders over the last few years.

Track record: Now, if I want to know about a person—if I were a therapist—one of the first questions I would ask is, "Tell me about your job history." That tells me a lot. On the whole, as my dad used to say, "People who get A's are smart." People who have a successful track record tend to be effective. We don't always go on that, because sometimes these people don't grow. But, if I had only one measuring stick, it would be that one: tell me your job history. Let's talk about whether it looks successful or whether you view it as successful or not. It's hard to define, but it's about whether or not you have the capacity a good curator or a good selector has to know people. It's always a tough one; God knows we all make mistakes. Your taste means your capacity to judge other people in relation to the other six characteristics.

I think taste and judgment are combined. I dealt with them separately because I thought taste was specifically the selection of people in an intuitive and objective way, but also in a subjective way. It has to do with the range of such things as being bold versus being reckless. It has to do with the strategic implications and consequences of any decision and what you take into account in making any decision, especially the tough ones. The easy ones are different; everyone looks good in a bull market. It's when things get tough, vulnerable, difficult, and in a crisis mode that judgment really counts the most. Taste and judgment are the hardest things to learn, let alone teach.

Character: Here I have in mind a variety of things such as size of ego, the capacity to listen, emotional intelligence, integrity, and authenticity. Basically, is this a person I can trust? That's what character is all about.

Wright

You said that businesses get rid of their top leaders because of lapses in judgment and lapses in character, not because of business literacy or conceptual skills. Why do you think this is true?

Bennis

It's true simply because it's true. Look at the record. I wasn't just stating a hypothesis there that looks to be proved. I was stating experiences with leaders and I'll give you three quick examples.

Howell Raines had the top job in journalism in the world. He had great ideas, great business literacy, and all the things in the top five. He did not have taste, judgment, or character. This is a guy who had an ego the size of Texas. He played favorites, had the best ideas, and was a terrific newspaperman—no one would argue with that. But, his way of treating people, of not harnessing the human harvest that was there, and his bullying, brutalizing, arrogant behavior, and his inability to listen; that's an example of lack of character.

Eckhart Pfeiffer was fired after seven or eight very good years at Compaq. He had terrific ideas, but he did not listen to people. He would only listen to those on his "A" list who were saying, "Aye, aye, sir." People on his "B" list were saying, "You'd better look at what Gateway and Dell are doing; they're eating our lunch on our best china." He didn't listen; he didn't want to listen. That's what I mean by character.

Let me just stay with those two examples, I don't think it's ever about conceptual abilities—ever. There may be some examples I just don't know about; but with over fifty years of leadership research, I don't know of any leader who has lost his or her job or has been ousted because of a lack of brainpower.

Wright

You said that teaching leadership is impossible, but you also said leadership can be learned. How can that be?

Bennis

Let me qualify that. I teach the stuff, so no, it isn't impossible to teach you. As is the case with everything, teaching and learning are two different things. One has to do with input into people; the other has to do with whether or not they get it. You know very well, and your listeners and readers know very well, that there's a difference between listening to a lecture and it having any influence on you. You can listen to a brilliant lecture and nothing may happen. So, there's a disconnect with teaching and learning.

Actually, how people learn about leadership varies a lot. Most people don't learn about leadership by getting a PhD or by reading a book or by listening to a tape, although these may be helpful. They learn it through work and experience. You can be helped by terrific teaching from a recording, a tape, a book, or a weekend retreat.

Basically, the way people learn about leadership is by keeping their eyes open, being observant, having good role models, and being able to see how they deal with life's adversities. You don't learn leadership by reading books. They are helpful, don't get me wrong. I write books; I want them to be read. The message you are trying to get out to people via the written word is important. I think it's terrific. That's my life's work. That's what I do for a living, and I love it. I'll tell you, it has to be augmented by the experiences you face in work and in life.

Wright

Trust me, I have learned, after reading many of your books, that they are teaching materials.

Bennis

Thank you. I hope you also learn from them, David.

Wright

As I was reading those books, I did the things you said to do, and they worked when I did it. The reason they worked is simply because I learned by doing.

Bennis

Thank you. I'm really glad to hear that.

Wright

Since leadership is where the big money, prestige, and power is, why would seasoned business executives, who are monitored more closely than the average employee, let character issues bring them down? An example would be a person who constantly uses profanity, deciding to just not curse in church.

Bennis

I wish it were that easy. It's a really good question. I wish I knew the answer, but I don't. I will give you a real quick example. Howell Raines, as I said before, executive editor of the *New York Times* (people would die to get that position) was an experienced newspaperman, and there was a 17,000-word article about him in *New Yorker*, June 6, 2002 (he had been on the job since September 2001, so it was written not a year later). The article exposed him; it was a very frank and interesting article. It called him arrogant, a bully, playing favorites—all the things I said earlier. It also called him a hell of a good man and a terrific editor. He'd been around the track; he had business literacy up the wazoo. He was as good as they get.

He read that article and everybody at the *New York Times* read it. Do you think it might have made him want to change a little bit? Did Julius Caesar not hear the warnings, "Beware the Ides of March?" Did he not hear, "Don't go to the forum?" There were so many signals and he wasn't listening. Why wasn't he listening? Didn't Raines go down to the newsroom and talk to those people? No. The most common and fatal error is that of arrogance—to stop listening. It could happen internally, as in the case of Howell Raines or like Eckhart Pfeiffer, who wasn't listening to his "B" list telling him about Gateway and Dell.

I don't have the answer to your question, but I will tell you, someone ought to be around to remind these people of the voices, stakeholders, and audiences they aren't listening to. That's a way of dealing with it—making sure you have a trusted staff that isn't just giving you the good news.

Wright

I've often heard that if I had been Nixon, I would have burned the tapes, apologized, and moved on.

Bennis

Absolutely.

Wright

I think it's the arrogance factor; you really "hit the nail on the head" when you said that, to put it in my simple terms.

How does one experience leadership when he or she hasn't yet become a leader?

Bennis

How do you become a parent for the first time? There's no book that you are going to read on becoming a parent any more than there is a book you are going to read on becoming a leader that will prepare you for that experience. You're going to fall on your face, get up, dust yourself off, and go on. The only thing you're going to learn from is your experiences and having someone around you can depend on for straight, reflective back talk. A lot of it is breaks, and chance. Some of it isn't that, but if there's one thing I want to underscore, nobody is prepared the first time they are going to be in the leadership position. You're going to fall on your face, you're going to learn from it, and you're going to continue that for the rest of your life.

Wright

At one time, I had a company with about 175 people working for me; we had business in the millions. I just kept making so many mistakes that afterward, I did wish I had read some of the things you had written about before I made those mistakes. It sure would have been helpful.

In your studies, you found that failure, not success, had a greater impact on future leaders—leaders learn the most by facing adversity. Do you think teachers at the college level make this clear?

Bennis

I can't speak for all teachers at the college level. Do you mean people teaching leadership and business management at the college level?

Wright

Yes.

Bennis

I don't know if they do. But, I would imagine things are much more difficult and complicated today because of the kinds of things that business leaders are facing such as: globalization, fierce Darwinian competitiveness, complexity of the problems, regulatory pressures, changes in demography, difficulty of retaining your best talent, the price of terrific human capital and then keeping them, the ability to help create a climate that encourages collaboration, and then there's the world danger since 9/11.

Wright

In my case, I just remember the equations and things in the courses I took, like controlling and directing and those kinds of things. I don't remember anybody ever telling me about exit strategies or what's going to happen if my secretary gets pregnant and my greatest salesperson is the one responsible for it. Which one do I fire? As the owner of a small company that's growing at a rapid pace, what can I do to facilitate the competencies of the people I have chosen to lead this enterprise into the future?

Bennis

Your company is how big, again?

Wright

I was talking before about a real estate conglomerate. Presently I have a speakers' bureau/servicing agency and a publishing business. I employ about twenty-five people, and we also use about fifty vendors I look at as employees also.

Bennis

Yes, vendors are, aren't they? That's a good way of thinking about it.

There are several things you can do in any size company, but with a small company, you can get your arms around it—conceptually, anyway. The leader/owner has to model the very behaviors he wants others to model. If you are espousing something that is antithetical to your behavior, then that's going to be a double bind. That's number one.

The second thing is to make leadership development an organic part of the activities at the firm. In addition to encouraging people to read, bringing in people to talk to them, and having retreats every once in a while, look at leadership competencies and what people can do to sharpen and enhance those capacities needed to create a culture where people can openly talk about these issues. All of those things can be used to create a climate where leadership development is a part of the everyday dialogue.

Wright

If you were helping me choose people to assume leadership roles as my company grows, what characteristics would you suggest I look for?

Bennis

I've implied some of them early on as we discussed those seven characteristics. I've become a little leery of the whole selection process; there is some evidence that even interviews don't give you really valid insight. I think what I would tend to do is look at the track record. Talk about that with potential employees—where they think they have failed and where they think they have succeeded. Try to get a sense of their capacity to reflect on issues and see to what extent they have been able to learn from their previous experiences.

See what you can make of how realistically they assess a situation. Most people rarely attribute any blame to themselves; they always think in terms of, "The dog ate my homework." It's always some other agent outside of themselves that is to blame. Those are the things that I think are going to be characteristics of emerging leaders among men and women. That's what I would look for—the capacity to reflect and learn.

Wright

When you made that comment about interviews, I don't feel as inept as I did before this conversation. I'm in my sixties and the longer I live, I just feel that when people come in and interview, I want to give them an Academy Award as they walk out. People can say almost anything convincingly in this culture. It's very, very difficult for me to get through, so that's one thing I really had not thought of. It seems so simple though—just follow the track record.

Bennis

I have had the same experience you've had. When I was president of the university and making lots of choices all the time, my best was hitting seven hundred, which means I was off three out of ten times. I think my average here was 60/40; it's rough. It's even harder these days because of legal restrictions—how much you can say about their references, how much they can reveal. We have to pay attention to selection level, no kidding. We can overcome mistakes in the selection level by the culture and how it will screen out behaviors that are not acceptable. That's our best default—the culture itself will so educate people that even mistakes we make will be resurrected by the culture being our best friend and ally.

Wright

As a leader, generating trust is essential. You have written extensively on this subject. Will you give our readers some factors that tend to generate trust?

Bennis

People want leaders who exude that they know what they are doing. They want a doctor who is competent and they want a boss who really knows his or her way around. Secondly, you want someone who is really on your side—a caring leader. Thirdly, you want a leader who has directness, integrity, congruity, who returns calls, and is trustworthy, who will be there when needed and cares about you and about your growth. Those are the main things. It's not just the individuals involved.

A boss must create a climate within the group that provides psychological safety—a holding pattern where people feel comfortable in speaking openly. I think that's another key factor in generating and establishing trust.

Wright

It is said that young people these days have less hope than their parents. What can leaders do to instill hope in their employees?

Bennis

All (and you can emphasize the word *all*) the leaders I have known have a high degree of optimism and a low degree of pessimism. They are, as Confucius said, "purveyors of hope." Look at Reagan; in a way look at Clinton, and Martin Luther King, Jr. These are people who have held out an idea of what we could become and made us proud of ourselves, created noble aspirations—sometimes audacious, but noble. Leaders have to express in an authentic way that there is a future for our nation and that you have a part in developing that future with me.

Wright

Dr. Bennis, thank you for being with us today, and for taking so much time to answer these questions.

Bennis

Thank you for having me.

About Warren Bennis

WARREN BENNIS has written or edited twenty-seven books, including the best-selling *Leaders* and *On Becoming a Leader*, both of which have been translated into twenty-one languages. He has served on four U.S. presidential advisory boards and has consulted for many Fortune 500 companies including General Electric, Ford, and Starbucks. The *Wall Street Journal* named him one of the top ten speakers on management in 1993 and 1996, and *Forbes* magazine referred to him as "the dean of leadership gurus."

Warren Bennis
m.christian@marshall.usc.edu

Chapter Three

An interview with...

R.G. Williams

Open Your Destiny

David Wright (Wright)

R.G. Williams is an active real estate investor, educational trainer, and one-on-one motivational mentor. He has been successfully investing in real estate for over ten years. Currently he invests nationally as well as internationally with properties ranging from single- and multi-family residences, to commercial properties and developments.

R.G. is a published author in Real Estate with training manuals, monthly articles in Real Estate magazines. He is a guest speaker to Investors Associations nationwide as well as Real Estate agencies and brokerages. He is a frequent guest on Real Estate Round Table and other syndicated television and radio shows. He was nominated to "Who's Who of Professionals."

R.G.'s mentoring specialties include but are not limited to: Real Estate, Business Consulting and Development, Personal Development, Financial Management, and Debt Freedom. He has been instrumental in the development of the coaching and training curriculum for Creative Learning Institute, Real Estate Investor Support, RESuccessgroup, and Dr. A. D. Kessler.

R.G. is adept at helping others achieve higher levels of success and dreams in their lives by helping them see things from a different perspective and keeping them accountable to those dreams and goals.

R.G. is CEO of Creative Real Estate Academy of Training—CREATE, a member of the Board of Directors for Invest in Kids, and co-founder of the Rosas Humanitarian Foundation, an organization that is building a hospital for the town of Lo Arado, Mexico.

Roger, welcome to *Success Strategies*.

Roger Williams (Williams)

Thank you.

Wright

Why is focusing on the "where" of your life more important than anything else?

Williams

Just the statement in and of itself—"the where"—throws people off. We have always been taught that we need to believe in ourselves. The challenge I have found is that most people do not take the time to find out who they are, therefore they run through life in a constant state of internal confusion and they don't even know why they are confused.

What I started looking at within myself was: 1) you need to define who you are, and 2) more importantly you need to define where you want to be—"the where" in your life. So, as I defined myself, my life, and "the where," I gained tremendous power over daily obstacles. The challenges that jump out at you every day lose their power over you because "the where" gives you what I call unwavering confidence. "The where" creates the spiritual strength that works from within, gives you internal drive, and prepares you emotionally for everything that crosses your path. Defining "the where" and working with a confident focus not only internalizes it, but mentally and emotionally you "get it." That pushes you beyond anything you could ever imagine. It is almost like climbing to the top of a mountain. When you get there you look around and think, "Wow, look at all the other opportunities that are out there for me!" Focusing on "the where" allows you the confidence to focus on what you are becoming and not on what you are.

Wright

Why do you say, "If money is all you are after, you most likely will miss your mark"?

Williams

To me money is simply a measurement of outside achievement. It is a way of keeping score. I have always said money is neutral. It doesn't care who owns it. It basically reflects a mirror image of who you are inside. Money makes good people great and bad people worse. What you do with money reveals everything. If what you focus the use of money on is not in harmony with where you are or who you are becoming, you will forever be in conflict within yourself. So the power is an understanding of where your life is, how you let it happen, and the true meaning of things that come from within. Money simply becomes a byproduct or an added bonus. In other words, money doesn't define you, it shouldn't define you, and the car you drive shouldn't define you. The clothes you wear, the house you live in, the watch you wear, and the pen with the star on the top should not define you. Yet society pushes in that direction and says that those are the things that do define us.

When you truly focus on being where you want to be and how you want to develop your lifestyle, money comes. It is similar to the dog chasing its tail—as soon as the dog realizes that all he has to do is go forward and his tail will follow, he can stop running in circles. So many of us run in circles chasing an unknown without ever getting anything or anywhere and then find out that once we get it, we don't know what to do with it. The sad fact is that what we get is too often not what we wanted anyway.

By looking at money instead of focusing on your mark, you will find yourself unfulfilled and confused as to why you feel that way. It is like driving down the freeway not knowing which exit to take and then wondering how you got to where you are.

Wright

How do you reverse engineer your life? Start with the end in mind?

Williams

I am always studying from others. One of the things I have learned from Stephen Covey is that you "begin with the end in mind." I never understood what that meant and I had a hard time breaking through the barrier of the meaning.

In a conversation I had with a client, the answer came to me. I was explaining how I had accomplished a certain goal and that is when it hit me—I needed to write down how I became and not how I was becoming! So, in other words, I needed to define the path I took to get there. Then, as I moved forward on my path, the steps were laid out for me and all I had to do was follow the steps.

Reverse engineering started with my definition of lifestyle and then worked back on how I had accomplished everything. Let's take a goal—you want to become a millionaire. It shouldn't be, "I want to become a millionaire," it should be, "How did I become that millionaire?" and then reverse engineer—put the steps together as to how you did it. This becomes your map or plan of action.

Wright

What do you mean when you say, "Treat money as numbers not lifestyle?"

Williams

This is where I have a lot of fun because, as I mentioned before, money is just an outside measurement. The challenge most people face is that they never take the time to define what money is and what money means to them. It is all a mental game.

We are brought up in a society that typically demands money. We never understand what money is. We go through school being taught how to make money, yet we are never taught what to do with money when we make it. We are not taught saving principles or how to spend wisely, so we never really have a concept about what money is. When you just simply ask yourself how to make money—a common question—the brain will think, "Special paper and ink is used, templates are created, then the U.S. Department of the Treasury, Bureau of Engraving and Printing, runs it through a special machine. The printed money comes out the other side, it is cut down and distributed for use." You have to be very specific and clear with the questions you ask yourself. Ask yourself empowering questions, such as: "How can I provide better for my family" or "How do I earn sufficient amounts to—" When you just look at money as money, you will see too many obstacles and your focus will be clouded. When you treat money as numbers, your focus remains clear because the emotional connection is removed.

Most people never take the time to define their life, therefore their focus becomes driven by material things only. Lifestyle covers every area of your life. When you look at all areas of your life powered by an understanding of "the where" in your life, you will then empower your dreams and goals into reality. Money will follow when you put your focus on your internal passion you will be more satisfied.

Letting money control the where and when of your lifestyle will lead you down a very lonely path and will leave you always wanting more.

Wright

Explain why it is important to have a mentor.

Williams

The meaning of mentor is "a wise and trusted counselor." It is simply giving back to others and what I realized is that I cannot do everything alone and I can only see so far.

Having a mentor in your life is having additional eyes looking out ahead as you follow your map and game plan. Everybody needs a mentor; Michael Jordan had five separate mentors. Alexander the Great had Aristotle who kept his game on the edge. Successful people throughout history consulted their mentors because doing so gave them a chance to step out of their game, use additional eyes, and then step back in and make that critical play or make a critical decision or what ever it was in their game.

When you are confronted with a critical situation a mentor simply keeps you on track. Mentors will also give you that gentle nudge or shove when you need it. You might feel that you are at the edge and you don't want to go through. A mentor is there to help you with those internal feelings and can help you make the best decision. Mentors are also there to be a friend and give you guidance.

Wright

Explain consistent action and constant work

Williams

Once you have a true heart-to-heart conversation with yourself regarding your dreams, passions, and goals it is then time to go to work. Consistent action means that you have a plan, you implement it, and when you begin to take action, you are doing the same thing over and over again. The repetition of simple things leads to an inevitable explosion. Constant work means that you remain true to your plan.

It is said that practice makes perfect. I disagree. I feel that "perfect" practice makes perfect. I could hit buckets of golf balls and while I am practicing my form could be completely wrong. I could have hundreds of hours on the golf course, but I will never hit like the greats simply because I never take the time to learn correct form. Learning what I must do to correctly swing the golf club, etc., combined with work or practice would move me light years ahead of the pack.

In life, if we do the same habit over and over again without fine-tuning it, we find that we have nothing more than the same habit. We simply find ourselves confused as to why we are at a point where we didn't want to be or thought we would be somewhere else.

I remember reading one of my notepads from years ago and found that I was far from my path because I had not fine-tuned my consistent action. The only place you find success before work is in the dictionary.

Wright

Why should you "Give credit where credit is due?"

Williams

I have always lived by the statement that you "put your ego in your pocket or check it at the door." You are who you are because of multiple influences upon you. I hear the statement "I am a self-made millionaire" and I chuckle inside because none of us can accomplish something like that alone. Whether we are selling products or services, somebody had to buy it. So you are never "self-made"—there is always somebody else involved in the process.

I believe that humility is your standing spiritually and poverty is a state of mind. You must give credit where credit is due because then you are keeping your ego in check. When your ego gets in the way it simply blows out the candle of your mind and allows chaos and confusion to set in; a confused mind is never productive. So by allowing the energy to flow back to those who participated in your game you are simply allowing the energies to help move you forward. You must always give credit where credit is due. If you are the one who created the opportunity, then by all means give yourself credit because that is where it is due.

Wright

How do you "act as if" you have already reached your goals?

Williams

It is like the assumptive close. When you are making a sale you should always use the assumptive close—"this sale is going to happen." Act as if your success is for certain. Act as if you have already accomplished the opportunity. "Act as if" simply means you are progressing with silent confidence with the assurance that what you have already put into play will be accomplished. Everything you committed to and defined in your heart-to-heart talks with yourself will come to pass.

Once you commit and act as if the energies and everything that surrounds you begins pushing you forward. Without acting with confidence that your future is secured, you allow for negative energies, fears, reluctance, and hesitancy to control your life. If you are playing half speed in the business world, or more importantly in life, then you are going to get hurt. The biggest frustrations come when you look back over your life and think, "If only I had done this—" or "What if I had done that—. Now it is too late!" Acting as if allows for more memories and allows you to accomplish more goals and dreams.

Wright

Why is it important to "manage your energy?"

Williams

Life is a marathon and not a sprint. However, there are certain windows of opportunities when you have to use bursts of speeds to get through. Much like a track-and-field meet, certain events require bursts of speed to accomplish the act and move you into a stronger position. Examples include relationships that you are hesitant to develop, deals that you are hesitant to ask for the close, etc. Defining your lifestyle—your "where"—allows you to manage your energy. Those definitions allow you to be prepared at all times and to know when and where to increase performance within yourself. Consistently working and constantly staying on task helps manage your energy as well, keeping you focused for the entire game.

Wright

Share with us what you mean when you say, "Truly define what 'wealth' is."

Williams

So many people confuse terms. They talk about being wealthy when in reality they are talking about being rich. Wealth comes in the form of healthy children, the ability to put your feet on the ground every day, friendships, quiet times with family, etc. That is true wealth. Riches come in the form of dollars and so many do not take the time to define these terms, once again allowing chaos and confusion to set in.

I believe that I am the wealthiest person in the planet and that is what gives me the inner confidence and strength to move forward in all areas of my life. Riches will be added as I choose to take advantage of opportunities. Truly defining wealth allows you to see that opportunities are plentiful when you stop to look around.

Wright

Why should one "pay it forward?"

Williams

I truly believe that a selfish person is one who seeks everything without purpose and thus blocks the flow of things. It is fantastic for us to seek after knowledge, riches, and relationships, but I believe that it is selfish for us to allow those things to stop with us and not flow through us. In other words, where much is given, much is expected. It is critical for us to understand that once something is learned it is our responsibility to share with others all we have learned.

A parent raising children has the responsibility to share concerns about danger, happiness, feelings, emotions, etc. I know that my parents did a phenomenal job in working hard to make my life full and provide more opportunities; they paid it forward to me. Now I have responsibilities to do the same for my children and for those I touch. If I sit back and hold all my wealth and riches, then I am being very selfish.

Receiving wealth and riches and then not allowing them to flow through you is very detrimental to internal growth. Paying it forward is simply "what goes around comes around—plus!"

About R.G. Williams

R.G. WILLIAMS is an active real estate investor, educational trainer, and one-on-one motivational mentor.

R.G. has been successfully investing in real estate for over ten years. Currently he invests nationally as well as internationally with properties ranging from single- and multi-family residences, to commercial properties and developments.

R.G. is a published author in Real Estate with training manuals, monthly articles in Real Estate magazines, guest speaker to Investors Associations nationwide as well as "Real Estate agencies and brokerages. He is a frequent guest on Real Estate Round Table" and other syndicated television and radio shows. He was nominated to "Who's Who of Professionals."

R.G.'s mentoring specialties include but are not limited to, Real Estate, Business Consulting and Development, Personal Development, Financial Management and Debt Freedom. He has been instrumental in the development of the coaching and training curriculum for Creative Learning Institute, Real Estate Investor Support, RESuccessgroup, and Dr. A.D. Kessler.

R.G. is adept at helping others achieve higher levels of success and dreams in their lives by helping them see things from a different perspective and keeping them accountable to those dreams and goals.

R.G. is the CEO of "Creative Real Estate Academy of Training—CREATE," a member of the Board of Directors for "Invest in Kids" and co-Founder of the "Rosas Humanitarian Foundation" an organization that is building a hospital for the town of Lo Arado, Mexico.

R.G. Williams
CREATE—Creative Real Estate Academy of Training
4535 W Sahara Ave., Ste 200
Las Vegas, NV 89102-3622
801.403.0053
creativewealth03@yahoo.com
www.createwealth.com

Chapter Four

An interview with...

Mark David

PONO
Creating Balance in Cultures of High-Demand

David Wright (Wright)

Mark David, President of The Mark David Corporation, has provided customized training programs to Corporate America for over twenty years. Mark has supported fortune 1000 companies with his practical and human approach to success. He specializes in performance consulting and developing highly effective customized training programs that target specific business challenges within an organization. Mark's strategies provide professionals with the tools they need to thrive in high-demand cultures and create increased balance and contentment. After all, a balanced and happy professional is a highly productive one. Mark believes that success is an inside-outside game and there is unlimited potential in all of us waiting to be unlocked. Mark brings about the best results by bringing out the best in people.

Mark, welcome to *Success Strategies.*

Mark David

Thank you so much.

Wright

Mark, I understand that the key ingredient to the success of your performance consulting, executive coaching, and customized training programs is that you are in the field with your clients on a consistent basis experiencing their reality.

Tell me, what do you see? Will you describe the climate facing business professionals today?

David

Absolutely. Today we are dealing with cultures of high-demand. What I mean by "high-demand" is that organizations are flattening out, downsizing, and many professionals have multiple jobs. Some have as many as two and three full-time jobs in which they are being asked to accomplish more aggressive goals in the same amount of time with the same amount of resources.

In addition, each professional is facing increased technology demands. I find that technological advances have allowed us to accomplish things we never thought possible, but with a price. It has also increased the demands on us. Instead of having more time, we are expected to accomplish more because technology has made it possible to continue to work 24/7, 365 days a year. We have created a business culture in which you go to work, then after the workday is finished, you go home and you can "plug in" and continue to work. It's unbelievably interesting; professionals are bringing their Blackberries (which are sometimes referred to as "crack berries" in corporate America) on vacation with them. In order to succeed in high-demand cultures, you have to take the time to re-energize in order to return to work and perform at your very best. Otherwise, your work and family life will suffer. When that happens, it's even more difficult to perform at your highest level. Even if professionals worked twenty-four hours each day, seven days a week for a year, their workloads would still be more than what they could actually produce.

So how do we succeed in this type of environment? First you have to realize and accept that business is *not* as usual. You can't outwork the workload or demands as you have in the past. So, if you can't outwork it, what do you do? Well, you have to out-think it; and how do you out-think the situation? The answer is you have to slow down to get ahead. This is where my clients think I'm absolutely nuts. They will say to me, "Slow down! Are you kidding me? Things are moving way too fast to slow down!" I understand that "slowing down to get ahead" sounds like an oxymoron. But when I recommend "slowing down" I mean that I want you to take time to think, preplan, and trust your instincts. Tap into your creativity and innovation. Come up with an idea, a recommendation, or a solution to solve the problem, not out-work the problem. The key is to get out of your own way. It's all about using your brain not your brawn.

We are performing in an era (and I know most people are aware of this) where knowledge is power. I think the key is applying that knowledge with laser-like focus. This means ruthless prioritization on what needs to be accomplished in order to yield the highest payoff in cultures of high-demand.

The problem is that in the past, many high-performers rose to their level of achievement by controlling everything. The invisible glass ceiling is that they can't control everything. In today's business culture, to rise to the next level of performance and succeed in cultures of high-demand, you must give up control to gain control.

Wright

In your opinion, what are the critical steps companies need to take in order to support employees effectively through times like these?

David

There are four basic steps that we as leaders of a team, organization, or company have to take in order to support our professionals effectively. The first step is to set clear expectations. I know, this is an overused concept and seems incredibly elementary, but the key is to deliver crystal clear expectations, not simply clear expectations.

Surprisingly, I have observed during my infield consulting sessions, a lack of crystal clear expectations being set from all levels of an organization. Unfortunately, so many leaders, managers, and coaches skip this very important basic step even though they are extremely bright and work for very successful companies.

The reason it is missed so often is because we are moving too fast. Many times it's human nature to assume that we are clear. After all, it sounds clear in our own mind. Miscommunication is the number one cause of mistakes and wasted time in business. But, the truth is, we don't slow down just enough to check and make sure we are understood. We must set clear expectations and manage to it. So, what do I mean by "manage to it"? Believe it or not, we can't set an expectation just once. We have to repeat our message or as I say, broadcast our expectation numerous times in creative, innovative, and most importantly in energetic ways.

High-demand cultures drain our batteries. There is so much to accomplish and we are being exposed to so much information. Your team members will feed off your energy and appreciate your clarity. The end result is tasks, expectations, and goals will be met successfully in the shortest period of time with high levels of job satisfaction.

The second step is setting up an accountability process where your team members clearly understand the expectation, they clearly understand the consequences (both good and bad) if the expectation is met or not met, and they understand the consequences up front versus after the fact.

I believe a great business leader is a great coach. Great coaches are involved while still leading the organization to the ultimate goal. The only way for a great leader to ensure the team's success is to create checkpoints where he or she can make sure everyone is on task, clarify any questions, and offer any insight that will support everyone in staying on track to accomplish the overall goals and expectations. Can you imagine a football coach having nothing to say during half time? It's not micromanaging. It's smart and extremely proactive leadership that builds business momentum and prevents wasted time firefighting. The good news is, it is basic stuff!

In addition, by setting crystal clear expectations and clear accountability processes upfront you will create a culture of "no fear." This means that your team members know exactly what needs to be done and what will happen if they are successful or unsuccessful in completing the task or expectation. There's no wasted time during the execution phase. This is the laser-like focus and clarity I was speaking about earlier. No fear fosters confluency. Confluency means that you and your team members have the ability to tell the truth without fear of vaporizing the relationship. You can discuss professional behavior without getting personal. Professional relationships based on honesty are much more productive. "Confluence" in *Webster's Dictionary* explains it as two rivers that merge together to form one river. This is a great analogy of a highly productive team and company. It describes a team that is on the same page and able to communicate and hold each other accountable as productively as possible. This is what's needed to thrive in today's corporate culture.

I was recently working with a client where the manager informed me that his company just reorganized. I said, "Okay, that's not unusual these days." But his situation was a bit unique because his span of control just increased five times in size. This manager would now be in charge of thirty-five individuals versus seven.

I said, "Wow, what an incredible jump in responsibility. This should make your career exciting." I then asked, "What type of support or plan did you receive to help you manage your new span of control?"

He answered, "Plan? No plan. It's all up to me to figure out how to handle it successfully. I already told my family that I won't be seeing them very often over the next six months."

Management delivered the goal/expectation but with no plan or accountability process to manage through the change of increasing five times the responsibility. These types of changes are eminent in corporate America. My advice to anyone facing this or a similar type of situation is save yourself and your team an enormous amount of wasted time and set everyone up for success. As the leader, don't just say, "Here's the change, now go do it!" Instead, reset the expectation, reset the accountability process, and provide your team members with a plan of execution to successfully meet the new expectation. You will save everyone so much time and effort.

The "just go do it" type of leadership in my world is totally Neanderthal, obsolete, and is not effective. Most importantly, you cannot call yourself a true leader if you don't provide a clear plan for success. This recommendation obviously doesn't hold true when we are under fire and we have to immediately pull a rabbit out of a magic hat. There are so many times when we can provide answers and let our team members expand upon those answers with better ideas. We want to ignite creativity and innovation within our team members.

The third step is setting up what I call, "water-cooler communication and feedback." As an effective leader, you have to pre-plan checkpoints when you will provide feedback and support. The most important element of these checkpoints is they are short in length, just like a chat at the water-cooler. Checkpoints open the door to making needed adjustments. We all know that any well thought-out plan may need adjustments. Providing your team members with the environment to receive proactive feedback and support will help them learn how to make the correct adjustments to stay on track and be successful in meeting your expectations. Be consistent with providing feedback checkpoints or "water cooler feedback" and your team members will expect and welcome your input.

The fourth and final step is yet another simple and well-known concept that we as leaders rarely have time to implement—Motivation. In cultures of high-demand, we have to find simple ways to motivate and re-energize our team members while on the job. Don't wait to conduct a team meeting on motivation or wait for your training department to deliver a workshop on motivation. Motivation is a critical part of every great leader's job description.

As I mentioned earlier, the current climate is draining our batteries. Our team members need to be motivated and re-energized on a consistent basis. The key motivator today is education. The good news is, this concept doesn't eat up your budget and can be implemented without taking a lot of your time. Your team members are seeking education that will help them perform their job responsibilities more proficiently. Believe me, your team members are screaming inside, "Teach me and show me how to perform my job better. Please! I need to learn how to accomplish more in less time."

Most team members have been programmed not to ask for help because corporate America will label them weak or dispensable. The fact is, the world is moving so fast, your team members need all the help they can get to achieve success.

Another effective way to motivate your team members is creating alignment between their personal goals and dreams to the job at hand. The bottom line is, the reason they are working is to achieve their personal goals. The company they work for and the job they currently hold is the vehicle to achieving their dreams. You only have to take a small amount of time to understand what each team member is working for whether it's a larger home, acquiring an MBA, more family time, or a trip to Hawaii. These are the reasons they work so hard. If you take the time to find out a few key reasons why they are working, you will be able to speak each team member's language and provide him or her with the motivation each one needs. Connect the expectation at hand to moving your team members closer to achieving their dreams. Leaders who motivate create loyal and hard-working followers. It's not magic—it is understanding how to motivate others.

In conclusion, you can support your team members in succeeding in cultures of high-demand by performing the basics such as setting crystal clear expectations, holding team members accountable, and providing consistent feedback and motivation. As I say to my clients, "Perform the basics brilliantly today and you will automatically ensure your success for tomorrow."

Wright

You speak a lot about creating balance in cultures of high-demand. What does that really mean in the business world? Why is it important?

David

When we look at handling our enormous workloads, maintaining balance is one of the most difficult yet critical tasks at hand. Effective prioritization is one of the most important skills we can master to create balance. We have to move away from "winging it" to a more strategic thinking and planning process.

First and foremost, you need to create a personal description of what balance means to you as an individual. Balance means something different to everyone. A word that I learned from Dr. Paul Pearsall, a Hawaiian heart surgeon, is *Pono. Pono* is the Hawaiian word meaning balance. When you travel to Hawaii and they put the lei around your neck and those beautiful flowers smell so wonderful and they perform a hula dance to greet you, it's all about *Pono.* The hula dance itself represents balance in life. Life goes up and down (just like the hula). Don't sweat the small stuff.

Pono is a concept that I have shared with my clients over the last few years. I ask each client, "How would you define balance in your life? What do you have to do to stay balanced at work, at home, and with yourself?" Once again we need to slow down to get ahead, think about what balance means to us, and clearly define balance/*Pono* in all areas of our life.

Following your passion or destiny can certainly create balance in one's life. Yet so many people are not born with an internal compass that says here is your life's purpose, here is your destiny, or here is the direction you should take. Then there are those like my dentist. I remember asking him, "When did you know you wanted to be a dentist?" He said, "Oh the first time I had my teeth worked on. I think I was about six years old."

Another example of the minority is Billy Crystal, the comedian. He knew he wanted to be a comedian when he was a very young child. His parents started videotaping him when he was four and five years old. He had a fake microphone and was performing stand-up comedy shows for his family.

Another great story is about Ted Williams. His mother begged his kindergarten teacher to please allow Ted to bring his bat to school. He in fact had his bat with him in class way back then. He knew he couldn't live without it and he knew he was going to be a baseball player one day.

These people are blessed. They are truly blessed because they clearly knew what they wanted to do with their life at a very young age. They knew without question that they wanted to be a doctor, a lawyer, an actor, etc. This passion and clarity keeps them more balanced than not because they are surely living their destiny.

The majority of professionals in corporate America are not like these individuals. They are capable in many areas and could make a good living in various professions. *Pono* helps you take a step back and define your life's destiny or accept the path you are on because it fosters what you want to achieve in your personal life. *Pono* starts with knowing what you want. *Pono* helps you find the passion in your current career. It helps you see that what you are currently doing is most important. *Pono* prevents you from being ripped apart internally or fragmented internally while performing your job and wishing you were an accountant versus a sales professional or an engineer versus a piano teacher. This fragmentation only leads to stress, unhappiness, and illness. Professionals today, need to seek out balance in order to be highly productive and live a healthy, long life.

Wright

What do you mean when you say, "Success is an inside-outside game"?

David

This philosophy directly relates to the concept of *Pono. Pono* is all about your "inside mentality." Becoming a balanced individual takes an internal focus. First, personally define what balance means to you. You also have to internally accept your current reality. Then it's time to "go inside" and develop your skill levels to become as productive as possible within cultures of high-demand and in all areas of your life. If the world continues to move faster and faster, the only place we can go to better our performance is inside ourselves.

The bottom line is, your outside world represents your inside world. In other words, you are on the outside what you believe on the inside. Every action you take, whether it's respectful or disrespectful, whether it's showing love or not showing love, your behavior on the outside is a direct reflection to what you believe you are on the inside. If you believe you are a loving, caring father, mother, wife, husband, son, worker, employer, then your actions will demonstrate that belief. When people ask me, "How can you know so much about me so quickly?" I say, "I'm observing your actions; I literally observe individuals as I would watch a silent movie." You should view yourself as a silent movie to determine what your actions say about you and your belief system. Actions represent the truth.

Professionals ask me all the time, "I need to become more productive and overall more successful. How do I change my behavior and/or my outcomes?" After they describe to me the specific changes they want to experience, I explain that it is not a matter of it just happening on the outside. You must first change your belief system, your self-esteem, your self-image, and your self-ideal in order to manifest these changes.

I use the following analogy: Imagine that inside all of us is an old three-drawer filing cabinet, dents and all. Inside the cabinet are different headings on hanging file folders such as work, family, and self. Within each hanging file folder are folders that hold descriptions of your pre-conditioned programs—how you act at work, with your family, and with yourself. You must go inside your internal file cabinet and identify and review all your programs that are pre-conditioned beliefs and behaviors and see what they tell you. If you don't like what the file says about your beliefs and behaviors, you just have to eliminate that file and replace it with the new file.

So, if your internal belief system is the key to your external results, how do you eliminate or replace unwanted beliefs? Once again, my answer is simple, basic, and proven, not only by me but by many experts in the field of success. The "magic wand" that I have discovered to changing your internal belief system is writing affirmations. You have to rewrite the programs in your file cabinet by writing down specific words and thoughts in the form of affirmations. These words represent what you think and want. You will create the new you with these precious words that you think about and act upon. For example: If you wanted to be a better husband and father to your family, you could write the following daily affirmation: "I am unconditionally loving my family with my actions and words. I look for opportunities daily to be a better husband and father. My family is giving me the opportunity to be the person I want to be every day and I act on it." This external act changes you internally, which then manifests the external results you desire.

Wright

Within your teachings you stress the importance of being in the "zone of productivity." How do you coach individuals to stay in their zone?

David

The key to getting into your zone is being, living, and working in the present moment of *now*. When I coach a professional to get into the *now,* I first make sure he or she is awake! We are moving so fast these days it's almost like we are spinning ourselves into a coma. To be awake and in the present moment of *now,* it means you are 100 percent conscious of the behavior you are executing; that means, no multi-tasking! It means listening to your Internal Voice of Reason, which I call your IVOR. Your IVOR will tell you if you are focused in the present moment of *now* or if you are stressing about the past or if you are anxious about the future. Once you are in the *now,* you are awake and you are conscious of your behavior.

The next step is to help process data through your Truth Filter. Imagine that we all have two filters in our brain that help us assimilate the enormous amount of data we receive on a daily basis. One is called the Ego Filter and the other is the Truth Filter. We must understand that all of us are making decisions based on our perception of what is happening around us and inside us.

I teach my clients to look through the Truth Filter to understand and see things for what they really are. Eliminate the emotion, the drama, and the judgment that the Ego Filter allows to come into play. The Ego Filter does not allow you to see or interpret data objectively. The Truth Filter allows you to see things for what they truly are. This is the key to making the correct decisions on a daily basis and maintaining "zone performance levels."

Eleanor Roosevelt said, "The quality of our lives is based on decisions we make." I absolutely agree with her. Being present in the moment of now, being awake, listening to your IVOR (Internal Voice of Reasoning), and looking at life through your Truth Filter is absolutely critical. All of this moves you into your state of *pono*/balance because you are looking at life objectively. If you see the truth, you can make the correct decisions. If you are making correct decisions, you are saving time each day.

Once your balance is in place, then and only then can you reach contentment. Contentment is complete happiness for self. Contentment means I'm in the right spot, right now. I'm at work because I want to be at work, I don't want to be on vacation, I don't want to be at home, I don't want to be at the gym, I want to be here at work. Or when I'm home, I'm not on the couch with my children and my family wishing I was in my virtual office, plugged in and responding to e-mails. You are content in the moment of now.

This is what I coach to my clients on a daily basis because I find that professionals are fragmented. Somehow we believe we can be in multiple places at one time. The truth is—you can't. It's impossible. You can only be physically in one place at one time. You can only really have one thought at a time and every time you fragment yourself you weaken yourself. This in turn increases your stress level, your anxiety levels, and you decrease your overall productivity.

As I mentioned previously, the only way to get into your performance zone—that place of effortless, flawless, highest level of perfection and productivity possible—is to stay in the now. You have to be awake. You have to be conscious. You have to listen to your IVOR (Internal Voice of Reasoning). You have to look at your entire world through your Truth Filter, not your Ego Filter. Then you are balanced. Then you are content.

Once you are content, you become a magnet that attracts health, prosperity, and success. There is a "drill" I recommend you perform to move yourself into the zone. Say to yourself, "I'm in the now. I'm awake. I'm listening to my IVOR. I have my Truth Filter up. I'm in a state of *pono.* I'm content. I'm in my zone."

Wright

What are some of your best time management tips to support business professionals in the following areas: work time, self-time, and family time?

David

Preplanning is the key to time management in all areas of your life, especially at work. We need to preplan our day, week, month, and year. Every Thursday, preplan your week in advance by outlining the goals and activities that need to be accomplished the following week. Don't ruin your weekend with planning on Sunday. Don't wait until Monday—you will lose so much time. Define what you need to accomplish over the next Monday through Sunday.

Preplanning saves you time because it takes less time to make an adjustment to a plan versus creating a plan each day when you are in a reactive mode. Review your plan for each day the night before and make any needed adjustments to stay on track for the week. The next morning, review your plan again. Things often change overnight and additional adjustments need to be made.

At this point you can let go and execute. Bring all of that enthusiasm and confidence to the table because you are clear and ready. You are absolutely ready to perform at your highest level because you've taken minimal time to create a well thought-out plan that attaches to what you want to achieve. It boils down to increasing your odds of achievement. Once you know what you want and you've created a simple plan, what you need to be accomplished will happen because it's a matter of execution and making adjustments.

When preplanning I strongly recommend that you eliminate your to-do list and convert it into an achieve list. An achieve list consists of the number one goal or task that needs to be accomplished that day/week. Once it's complete, then you can add four more items to your list. Once that's accomplished, you can add five more things to be accomplished. This is a much more productive way to accomplish your daily and weekly goals. Get rid of the marathon list of things to accomplish in one day, when it's humanly impossible.

Most professionals go home after a hard day's work and feel like failures since his/her to-do list is only 25 percent complete and they didn't accomplish the most important item. In our world it's all about accomplishing your most important goals and tasks first each day. So your achieve list should consist of your number one goal for the day/week, plus your number four goals for the day/week, plus your number five goals for the day/week. By accomplishing these priorities you will be more than ahead of the game. In addition, you will have created a wonderful feeling of self-motivation and self-accomplishment. This alone will provide the energy you need to succeed in high-demand cultures.

Regarding self-time, you must deliberately preplan time for yourself. You must be selfish and give time to yourself each day. So many of us are unconditionally giving and giving and giving and giving and we end up putting ourselves last. Yet, we are the energy source that our families, our employees, our communities draw upon.

How are you reenergizing yourself? What are you doing to keep yourself energized and healthy physically, mentally, and spiritually? Outside stimuli from coffee doesn't count! Identify a way to energize yourself. Whether it is running, reading a book, taking an hour and a half lunch break, going to the park, meditating, reading to your children, holding your spouse's hand, or taking a dance class, you need to find one constructive activity to support yourself in maintaining total health and sanity. If you don't preplan time for yourself, it won't happen. Put yourself first. Being selfish in this manner is smart for you and for all the people who depend upon you.

Lastly, regarding family time, communication is critical. Ask your family members how they would like you to communicate with them. With over twenty years of coaching powerful professionals within corporate America, I see and hear it time and time again—your family wants you. They want time with you. They want you present in the now with them. If you haven't figured that out yet, hear it from me. They don't want your money—they don't want all the accessories that money can buy—they want you. Give them the one thing that money can't buy and that is your time.

Identify and preplan (there is that word again, preplan) specific family time. No matter how limited it is, let your family count on that time with you. I guarantee you there is more time to give. Review your calendar for the last three months. Discover where the windows of opportunity and small pockets of time are to spend more time with your family. Learn from the past and create the time and commitment going forward. Remember, great leaders make the invisible visible.

Most importantly, when you're there spending time with your family, truly be there. Don't be thinking about work. Be in the present moment of now. Be awake. Be in that state of contentment because they (especially if you have younger children) will know whether or not you are truly present.

Wright

What a great conversation! Personal and professional balance is very important isn't it?

David

It really is and the only way to get there is staying in that productivity zone as much as possible. It is the only way. I believe professionals can holistically have their cake and eat it too. It all goes back to truly defining what balance means to you and what beliefs you have filed in your internal filing cabinet.

Here's a quote from a fellow named Danny Cox. He said this many years ago: "If you go to work to pay your bills, you will always stay poor. If you go to work to pay for your dreams, your bills will always get paid."

It just doesn't happen for 99.9 percent of the population. We all have to work really hard to find and define what our internal map is. When you do find it and follow it, you become enormously successful. But so many professionals say they don't' have the time and they don't have the energy or they give up and go wherever the wind of the culture takes them. Often they end up in a job where they can do well and make tremendous money, but they are not really happy.

I believe as human beings, we must find out why we are here. The good news is that many individuals are in the right spot at the right time, they just don't know it. That is why I lead everyone into the now and tell them to wake up! Wake up and realize where you are and maximize your life. Life consists of work, family, and self. It's all interwoven and you, as do I, need to understand that no one is coming to save us and no one is coming to give us the answers about our internal filing cabinet. We each have that incredible responsibility, and once we unlock that cabinet, once we realize no one is coming, we will take on the responsibility and create a fantastic life filled with pono and contentment.

Wright

Well Mark, I really appreciate the time you've spent with me answering these questions this afternoon. I have learned a lot and I am positive that our readers will also. Any further pearls of wisdom you'd like to leave with our readers?

David

Yes, I have one last concept I'd like to share. It is the concept of "Boring is Good!" This concept has had a positive impact on the personal and business lives of many of my clients. The older I get, the more I want to hear, see, and experience life being a bit boring, uneventful, and predictable with no surprises when it comes to safety, health, family, friends, clients, and time.

Understand that it is okay to slow things down. There is no reason to rush the calmness and the beautiful feeling of "all is well." I challenge everyone to welcome and look forward to being bored. In these quiet times, you will find opportunities to create and appreciate *pono.*

Wright

Today we have been talking with Mark David, President of The Mark David Corporation. His company provides customized training programs, executive coaching, and performance consulting services to corporate America, all of which support behavioral change to accomplish increased results. As we have found today, he believes that success is an inside-outside game and there is unlimited potential in all of us just waiting to be unlocked.

Mark, thank you so much for being with us today on *Success Strategies.*

David

You are very welcome. Thank you so much for having me today. I so look forward to our next conversation.

About Mark David

IN 1987, MARK DAVID founded The Mark David Corporation. Mark combined his experience and talent as a successful turn-around expert and natural born executive coach to create a boutique training company. With his keen ability to uncover productivity roadblocks, Mark develops customized training programs and provides performance consulting sessions that target specific business issues.

Mark has guided individuals and Fortune 1000 companies to increased performance and profit through his practical and human approach to success. Mark specializes in providing key strategies to help today's professionals thrive in high-demand cultures.

Mark is the author of *Coaching Illustrated, The Self-Manager Success Journal,* and a full line of unique productivity tools in the areas of sales, goal planning, and leadership.

Mark David
The Mark David Corporation
23 Kelton Court
San Mateo, CA 94403
800.410.2677
mark@markdavid.com
www.bottomlinecoaching.com

Chapter Five

An interview with...

John Moser

Thoughts of a Leader

David Wright (Wright)

John Moser is a twenty-eight-year veteran of the professional training, development, speaking, and consulting world. He joined the world's largest international training organization as a sales associate in Washington, D.C., in 1978 following a career spanning six years as a professional golfer and member of the PGA. From 1980 to 1984 he was the number one salesperson worldwide and then he was promoted to run the Leadership Institute of Washington, D.C., for eight years before forming his own training, coaching, consulting, and speaking organization.

Because of his vast experience and notoriety, John was invited to the White House in preparation for sending President Regan to the Russian Summit. While in D.C. he was an annual trainer for the Defense Intelligence College and War College for twelve consecutive years.

Additionally, he was a former host of several live call-in radio shows including WERC *Street Talk* and WCEO *Monday Morning Sales Meeting.* He has appeared on a number of radio and television shows including Fox, NBC, ABC, and various cable networks. He regularly has articles published in regional and national newspapers and magazines including *Smithsonian, Business to Business, Personal Selling Power,* and editions of the *Business Journal.*

Some additional clients include several beauty pageant winners including the former Miss Alabama, Virginia, Maryland, and Miss America, six professional sports teams, IBM, ATT, Marriott, Cameron Valves, Parisians, O'Neal Steel, Merrill Lynch, First Protective, Oracle, Baptist Health Systems, NASA, FBI, Department of Agriculture, Mercedes-Benz, and over seventy-eight police and sheriffs' departments throughout the United States. Subjects include Leadership, Management, Executive Development, Sales, Service, Presentations, Communications, Change, Marketing, Teamwork, Motivation, Coaching, and Attitude.

John was born in Germany and attended college in Kentucky and Maryland.

John, welcome to *Success Strategies.*

John Moser (Moser)

Thank you David, I look forward to having this time with you.

Wright

It looks like you've done a lot of things in your life having to do with business.

Moser

I have, I've been fortunate over the last thirty years to be exposed to a lot of different leaders with a lot of different styles. Whether it was through the military, sports, or your day-to-day professional people, the opportunity was there to learn from them.

Wright

I remember that I was in a meeting with you recently where everybody at the table was more interested in your having been a golf pro. That must get some real good comments.

Moser

It does; it makes it a bit easier, but it also gave me the background to allow me to come from a competitive environment. Business is competitive, just like any sport is. Playing professional golf I had to understand that sometimes I was out there on my own, yet I had to rely on other people. When I entered the business world, my coaches and caddies were other business people. In business, coaches and caddies are as important as the players.

Wright

Where does leadership begin?

Moser

We often hear people refer to someone as a "born leader." I look at leadership and think about it in a different perspective—leadership is not a science or art; if it were, you would do exactly the same thing and get the same results every time. Sometimes people talk about it being an art—a skill—that you either have or you don't. I think there are characteristics required to be an effective leader like confidence, passion, and good communication skills. I believe leadership is a skill that may come at an early age from your parents, church, school, family, or coaches and mentors; but it develops over a period of time.

I think that people make a mistake when they see someone who is confident, passionate, or a good communicator and they think that person would be a tremendous leader. Those are great characteristics for leadership, but they don't necessarily always make someone a good leader. I think leadership is a combination of things that develop over a period of time—who and what a person has been exposed to, how the person has been challenged, and a person's natural traits.

You probably know better than anybody else that you can't necessarily judge a book by its cover. That is a mistake made by many people.

Wright

What impact does self-confidence and self-esteem play in being an effective leader?

Moser

When we look at confidence or self-esteem we look at the world we live in. When we find people who have a high level of confidence or self-esteem they are probably more flexible and they can generally give credit to others. They don't have to be in control of everything so they are able to delegate and give growth opportunities to others. They really enjoy watching people grow and receive credit for their efforts. They can let people around them be responsible and flourish.

The opposite is someone who is scared, who maybe has risen to a position well above what he or she is able to do. These people slow down things, they want to have control of everything, and they don't want to give credit to others. I think that even though those who have self-confidence and self-esteem might be loud, outspoken, and high strung, it doesn't necessarily mean they are confident people.

I think self-confidence and self-esteem are crucial qualities for a future leader because of certain changes taking place. For example, it used to be older people were teaching the young. Now the roles are reversed. People who are not very confident will struggle with that situation.

Wright

How do leaders think? Do they think differently than most people?

Moser

When I think of effective leaders I see them as builders for tomorrow. People are put in leadership positions for a lot of different reasons. An effective leader builds others, whether it's a mother building a child, a coach building a player on the field, or a supervisor building his or her team. These leaders become catalysts. They are thinking about tomorrow versus today.

I find that effective leaders are thinking, "Okay, what can I learn from yesterday, how can I get through today, and, more importantly, what's tomorrow going to look like?"

Look at the technology issues we have, and look at the ethnic and culture issues that are out there. There are going to be a lot of different problems to solve, so how do we handle tomorrow? Good leaders are always trying to help others succeed and compete.

One of the goals of leadership is to build systems, processes, and people so that they can accomplish tomorrow's objectives.

I hear of many businesses that are so consumed with what happened yesterday that they miss the opportunity for tomorrow. When tomorrow comes they are fighting for it because they didn't take time to prepare and to plan for it.

A good leader is really thinking of the future.

Wright

How do globalization, generational differences, and culture influence how you lead?

Moser

Well, especially in today's environment I believe there is so much diversity that the role of a leader must be flexible. My father was a general in the military and I grew up in a control and command environment. Therefore, my leadership style is more direct. But I've had to adapt, as others in leadership roles will have to. When you're dealing with different cultures, nationalities, or generations, one has to adapt to these situations. This will change the way you communicate, motivate, or interact with people as a leader.

In addressing generational differences, I mentioned younger adults in leadership roles rather than older adults. Technology may play an important role in how the former may lead, which could intimidate those less familiar. So I believe generational differences, culture, and globalization all play a tremendous role in the way we'll lead in the future.

Wright

How do most people attain a position of authority? How is this different than being in a leadership position?

Moser

People given positions of authority could have attained it through longevity and/or dedication to their company. Another might have passed a test or achieved a particular skill. For example, a worker on an assembly line who can produce a certain product faster/better than anyone else. Also, because of his success a top salesman is moved into a position of authority. The challenge with this is that just because good salespeople have had past success doesn't necessarily make them good leaders. Often they are given their position by others because of their skill set, not necessarily by their proven track record of being able to build, grow, and motivate other people, which is important for leaders.

People so often find themselves in a position of authority because of past accomplishments. However, this does not guarantee they will be good leaders.

Wright

How do personal values, character, and ethics play out in leadership?

Moser

There aren't too many days that go by where people are not influenced by their values, character, or ethics. I liken this to a tree. A tree has leaves, branches, a trunk, and roots. So often we judge people based on what we see and what they have—their car, schooling, clothes, or position. Then we look at the "trunk of the tree"—their skills or abilities. What we don't see are the "roots"—their values, character, and ethics.

Here's an example: On television, unfortunately, we see crimes of homicide or theft. The news reports will include an interview with a neighbor of the alleged murderer or thief. The neighbor might say, "I've known Joe for twenty years," or, "I've known Steve for thirty years, I can't believe he would do something like that." The fact is, the neighbor didn't know the accused at all. The neighbor has seen the person from the outside but didn't understand the person's values, character, beliefs, or ethics. The neighbor didn't understand the root system that the person really had. When you see reports on television or hear reports on the radio today, remember that character, beliefs, and ethics come into play.

A long time ago in Washington, D.C., I was watching a man build a building. He was looking at the granite and he said that the granite has integrity. I said, "What do you mean it has 'integrity'?"

He said, "John, it's real simple—it will stand the test of time."

A leader's decision, character, ethics, and beliefs are going to play out.

In contrast, the things you can see and hear on television today would have been considered X rated and unacceptable ten to fifteen years ago. Those things have influenced the thinking of the new leader of today—it is acceptable to see fighting on a baseball field or see a whole football team fight or to watch their political, business, and religious leaders engaging in any number of white collar crimes. Ethics, character, and values will play a roll because if leaders don't have a good foundation, it's going to show up in the way they manage and lead other people.

Wright

Do a leader's actions impact the engagement or disengagement of employees?

Moser

Many companies and people are talking about building, attracting, and retaining staff. Companies are saying that they are going to use "top grading" or use the "Good to Great method" or "get more A players." Very few are thinking about what leaders or people with authority do to either engage or disengage people by their actions. Do they make people feel devalued? Do they create unnecessary stress and overwhelm others? Do they create trust?

Leaders' interactions can have a significant impact on the environment they create. They should create an environment that allows people around them to really want to be involved, feel worthwhile, feel important, and to be excited about going to work. How many times do you hear someone say, "Gosh, I'm stuck in this job. If I could go back and start over I wouldn't do it."

If you add up the number of years and hours you've worked, starting at age eighteen through age sixty-five, at eight hours a day, five days a week, you've worked well over ninety thousand hours. If you're going to work that long, you ought to enjoy it.

I believe that a leader can create an exciting environment or can disconnect and destroy it by his or her interactions with others.

Wright

What happens when the leader's life is out of balance?

Moser

Today many people find themselves out of balance for a variety of reasons. They might be overwhelmed with travel, traffic, technology, sports, downsizing, or companies reorganizing and restructuring. In any position such as head of a household, ball team, church group, classroom, or business environment, if leaders don't have some balance with their family life, health, spiritual, community, and social life, or they are currently spending a great deal of time commuting to and from work, they will feel overwhelmed. The speed of business and the demands of life with e-mail and cell phones that people think they have to respond to right away can cause them to get out of balance.

For example, think about your car—when you are riding down the road and your car tires get out of balance there are two or three things you typically do: you can either slow down, speed up, get it fixed, or let it go. If you let it go, one day it will break down.

When we are out of balance, it influences the way we interact with others. We don't think as clearly, we are not as creative, and we certainly don't use the best interpersonal skills. My own belief is that if an organization can find some way to help their leaders have a better-balanced life, it will benefit the entire company.

I believe we are expecting increasing results from people and technology. Technology has given us ways to do things quicker and that has contributed toward creating an imbalance. Have you ever known people who can't go on vacation without checking their e-mail, voice mail, and text messages? It's reasonable to assume that these people are out of balance.

When we get out of balance, something eventually breaks; we will say and do things we shouldn't say and do. Remember, people are the greatest commodity. People touch every part of a business and life. If leaders are out of balance, pretty soon they can ruin some of those people.

Wright

How does technology influence one's ability to lead?

Moser

Technology, such as text messaging, the Internet, cell phones, and e-mail are all creating the need for speed, seven days a week, twenty-four hours a day. People expect things instantly. It used to be that you could get somebody a quote and take some time doing it. You could follow up with a letter, make a phone call, or set up a meeting.

Bill Gates said to me, "It's funny—I'll have people who will send a text message or e-mail to somebody five cubicles away rather than walk around and talk with them."

This kind of technologically created, hectic speed produces some issues with what we do and how we do things. The expectations are *I need it yesterday*. This doesn't allow people to interact. Technology also changes the way we work. Right now, during this interview, you and I are in two different states—you are in Tennessee and I am in Florida. Because of technology I can e-mail you something in moment or two. Today, because of technology, we can get a lot more information quickly. Everyone is expected to have that same level of understanding, which means we must constantly be out there learning.

Wright

What can a leader do to enhance communication among people?

Moser

First, an effective leader should recognize the various forms of communication. Today, the Internet dominates in this area but nonverbal communication can be interpreted differently. I still think human interaction, face to face, is crucial. We've got to find time to be able to talk, to make sure that people don't lose their interpersonal communication skills. I don't need to be a good listener if you are sending me text messages or you're sending me e-mails. I don't need to worry about my interpersonal skills because it's all on a piece of paper.

In order to interact more effectively at meetings, performance reviews, or being creative, leaders should expect their people to recognize that communication is crucial. Leaders should make it mandatory to allow people to talk and listen or there will be problems in the way that they do business on an ongoing basis.

Wright

There are many studies about communication styles, personality types, and behaviors. How can today's leaders leverage this information?

Moser

Your question is right on track. There have been a lot of research and studies done about communicating, learning styles, and personality and behavior types. This research has made understanding others easier. We all have blind spots. We must understand how communication impacts human behavior and how communication and behavior are linked together.

There are enough diagnostic tools out there that will help people understand the way they speak, process information, learn, think, and the way that they interact. Donald Trump has a totally different style than an engineer or an accountant—he likes control, directness, quick results, power, and short answers. Somebody who may be an engineer or an accountant would want more information, perfection, detail, and he or she may want to take time to work on answers. People need to recognize their personality style, the way they approach people, and the way they look for outcomes. In communication there should be a goal, whether it is to inform, to explain, to convince, or to teach. The goal is: "How do we best share that information?" If you use the assessment tools available, you are going to be able to inspire and direct others in a much more effective fashion.

Wright

Motivation—is it the leader's responsibility or the employees'?

Moser

It is interesting—there are various forms of persuasion and motivation. There are two schools of thought on this subject. There are some people who will say that it's the leader's responsibility to motivate employees and others will say that it's the employees' responsibility to motivate themselves. I think that in certain situations both of those answers are correct.

What I believe is that a leader can create the environment that allows people to be able to succeed and grow in a positive way. As an example: identical twins are different. If an organization wanted to motivate identical twins, even though they are "identical," they don't think, act, or respond the same and yet most organizations will treat them the same way. But they are individuals as well. It's leadership's responsibility to create an environment that allows people to succeed and grow individually and to recognize that people do things differently.

The key is to create an environment of appreciation. I don't mean just slapping them on the back or patting them on the head, but truly make people feel that it's okay to fail, to know that they'll be rewarded, and to make them feel worthwhile. The result of creating this kind of atmosphere may surprise you.

Wright

What actions and behaviors do leaders employ to influence and facilitate change?

Moser

A friend of mine was at Oxford doing a study on change and change management. He commented that there is so much written about change. We will change sometimes out of necessity. An example is a visit to the doctor. The doctor might say that if you don't stop smoking or drinking and if you don't start exercising or losing some weight, you won't live very long. The doctor's advice should cause the patient to change and the advice given should be motivation, at least for a short period of time, for the patient to change.

A leader must be willing to learn. If you are not willing to learn you are probably not willing to change. Just because something was done one way yesterday doesn't mean it has to be done that way today or tomorrow.

This goes back to the level of confidence that we talked about earlier. A leader has to be able to say that there may be different ways to do things. Leaders should encourage people to approach them with new methods and procedures.

I think change comes with learning and learning comes with the ability to admit that we don't know everything and we're willing to try things differently.

If you can create the atmosphere that allows a person to want to grow, you will create an environment that allows people to want to change.

I remember years ago when Dr. Deming was alive. I had a chance to spend two days with him. Everyone said that he was so passionate about the processes and systems; he was also concerned about people and their development. He said that if a person were willing to change and willing to learn, the organization would to be able to grow.

Wright

Leadership, like golf, has many different "tools." Explain why it's important to be skilled in using more than just one.

Moser

As a seasoned golfer, one may become comfortable with a certain style of play. For example, if you were going to chip around the green, there are some people who will always chip with a pitching wedge. It doesn't matter what the circumstances are, that's their favorite club—it's the one they think works best in *all* situations, so regardless as to whether or not there are other methods, they are not comfortable or willing to even except coaching.

The same goes with a longtime leader. If a person feels that the only way to deal with things is using a confrontational, direct approach, the person is limiting his or her ability to deal with the situation. People who think this way may say they have to show who's in charge. It's important for leaders to be flexible and open to new ideas.

Wright

Can you really be effective without passion as a leader?

Moser

I would say no and then I will define what "passion" means to me. I believe people confuse energy, loudness, and excitement with enthusiasm. You don't have to be an outwardly enthusiastic, bouncing-off-the-wall type of person to be passionate; but you must have a passion and excitement internally to be really effective. It doesn't matter whether it's about learning, family, friends, career, or sports, I don't care if it's about winning, money, teaching, or technology, there has to be something that drives you internally that creates a fire inside of you. If you are not passionate about it then you will not try to do better; you will not try to grow or share that passion with others. There aren't a lot of people who are very successful who don't have a passion—a "fire in their belly."

How often do you see people put into a sales position and then someone else comes along and says that he or she would be good at selling because that person is very enthusiastic or has a passion for that particular product or service? As a leader in that situation, I would much prefer to use a person who is passionate about that position.

I'm not talking about external energy here—I'm talking about that inner fire. David, you are passionate about your speakers' group and your publishing services. Your enthusiasm makes it easy to listen to you—it inspires others. Because you have that passion, you're willing to put forth effort and it comes out in the end product.

Wright

Many people think most meetings are a waste of time. What should a leader do about that?

Moser

We are using more technology these days and we may have fewer face-to-face meetings. One of the things that a leader can do is to make sure that meetings are fun and effective. Consider changing the format of the meetings. Ask people what they like or dislike about your meetings. Maybe you should set up some basic guidelines. Try these few questions at the end of your next meeting: What is working? What's not working? What is missing? What do you wish we would start or stop doing? Be willing to step out and change some things. Also, you'll find that there are people who shouldn't be there. Sometimes there are key departments or people missing. You want to make sure that you've got the right people doing the right things in those meetings. Rotate who conducts the meetings, get others more involved, request honest feedback, and change the format, or change who attends.

If the leader is willing to make changes, the meetings will improve.

Wright

In life there will always be conflict and disagreement. Tell us how effective leaders handle these situations.

Moser

There is always going to be conflict. An effective leader has to make sure that he or she understands. Leaders should realize that sometimes the person with the power can be in control. They have to realize that when there is conflict it has a direct impact on a person's attitude, either positively or negatively. The conflict may impact people's commitment level to the team or the organization and if it goes for a long time without being resolved there will be trouble. If the problem isn't resolved in the minds of the people involved and if they feel the situation was handled unfairly, it can cause them to disengage or completely disassociate, forcing them to look for other opportunities.

Leaders must make sure that they watch their personality style, and understand how others receive and process information so that when they're approaching others they are using their best interpersonal skills. They then recognize who's got the power and make sure that their rights are protected. People should leave the situation feeling that a positive resolution for both sides has been reached and that it was done correctly, completely, and in a timely manner.

This also goes back to confidence and communication skills. If a leader has confidence, he or she doesn't have to be right all the time. Self-confidence empowers leaders to sit down, listen, ask the right questions, and control their emotions. This keeps their team more engaged, safer, productive, and positive versus disengaged.

Wright

We all hear about the power of praise and recognition. How does it create a legacy for leaders?

Moser

If you were to ask people to name someone who had a significant influence on them, you will generally find that those individuals differ in size, shape, age, relationship, and position. One of them might have helped them when their bike fell over. One may have supported and encouraged them on the ball field or in the gym. The person may include a mentor, a boss, or a coworker, a friend, or family member. What those people did was create a legacy. When people reflect someone who had tremendous influence or impact on their life, it's usually because of that person's encouragement and support along the way.

A lot of people are trying to build a legacy with money, position, fame, or with their business. Consider the actions you take throughout your career and life in building, inspiring, and influencing other people. That creates a real legacy. You may not ever know the number of people throughout your life that you touch and who are where they are today due to the praise, support, encouragement, and recognition given by you in a sincere manner at the right place, in the right way, and at the right time.

I can tell you that praise and recognition have to be done with discernment. If you praise certain people in public they may not like it. If you give some people a letter, it may inspire them. So recognition is powerful.

Wright

How do effective leaders transition from being the star player to a championship coach?

Moser

I will share a story with you. When I was in Birmingham, Alabama, Michael Jordan was playing baseball for the Birmingham Barons; he had just come off a couple years' leave from the Chicago Bulls. I had a chance to chat with him and I asked, "Why do you think you were picked to be the coach of the Washington Bullets basketball team? Was it due to your coaching abilities or your basketball abilities?" Michael's answer had a lot to do with being a team player.

You've got to be willing to let other people have the credit. You've got to be willing to understand that just because you do it a certain way doesn't mean that's the only way.

So it's a challenge going from start player to championship coach. My recommendation would be that when people are looking at taking a star player and make him or her a coach or supervisor, they need to recognize the qualities that person has and decide if that person is actually able to do the job.

Consider the challenges you find in business. A great salesperson will be moved to a sales manager's position. How does that person become a great coach or supervisor? Accomplishing this can be difficult because he or she has always been recognized on an individual basis. The success of good salespeople is based on their own individual efforts and performance. When they become managers, they must transition from achieving individual success to achieving success leading a team. As managers, they are only successful when their team is successful.

I know personally that this is a challenge. It was a challenge for me when I went from being one of the top salespeople in the world to leading a team. At first it was very difficult to sit in an auditorium or convention center and have my people receive the recognition I used to receive.

To be a top performer you have to work hard on your own and depend on yourself. To be a good coach or supervisor, you have to depend on a lot of people and work well with them. That's a challenging transition. For me, I finally made it and it was because many people helped me.

Wright

Do great leaders have mentors and coaches?

Moser

Certainly. If we consider professional and collegiate sports, business professionals, singers, dancers, actors, musicians, beauty pageant participants, and Olympic athletes, you will see many different coaches and mentors. Let's look at Tiger Woods. He may have a variety of coaches. He probably has mentors and coaches he works with, whether it's working with his short game or a personal trainer, a swing coach, a caddy—maybe he even consults a psychic.

I believe that great leaders have to find people who can mentor, guide, assist, or coach them. It doesn't have to be a paid coach from the outside. It can be somebody they talk to, someone they spend time with who allows them to recognize if there are any gaps in the way they do things. I look at our Olympic athletes who are going to compete. They have many great coaches who work with them in a variety of areas. If you consider singers and dancers, most have many great coaches who work with them.

In business, because of people's egos, it's hard for them to be able to admit that they need some help unless they are confident. If you are a superstar you generally feel that you can do it on your own. If your confidence isn't as high as it should be, you won't want anyone to give you advice. If you're not good at communicating or you're lacking interpersonal skills, you need to be able to go to other people and say, "Please help me!"

Imagine yourself with your first child. You'd need someone to help you understand child rearing. Just because you had the child doesn't mean you know what you need to know to raise the child. Most people ask for help along the way.

Wright

What impact does a leader's attitude have on people's motivation, learning, morality, and growth?

Moser

A question I ask is, "Do people believe attitude has an impact on learning, motivation, relationships, and communications?" In most groups I speak to, nearly 90 percent will say that a person's attitude influences the way he or she deals with people and how the person is motivated, and that creates the environment. When you say about someone, "That person has an attitude," is that generally a positive or negative statement? Almost every time it's considered a negative statement.

Yet attitude is one of those things you can hear and sense even through the phone line. You can tell if someone is having a good or bad day. You can see it on someone's face. It determines whether you want to approach that person or not. I find that it's the one thing we have a real chance to control, regardless of where we are born or what takes place. Attitude is the one thing that most people fail to protect and strengthen. They let circumstances impact it and yet most will say that they have control over their own attitudes.

I believe a leader's attitude has far more impact and influence than most believe and if a leader has a negative, positive, or disruptive attitude it will impact everyone that leader comes in contact with. If the leader has a negative attitude, there will be a lot of people slipping during that day.

Wright

Why must leaders develop the skills necessary to become effective coaches?

Moser

A leader's job is to build people. Effective coaches study the past. They review films and have after-actions meetings. An effective coach realizes that people have different skill sets, different abilities, and are motivated by different things. Coaches have to be prepared from a succession perspective. They have to consider the age of the players—some may be getting older and some may get injured. They're always planning ahead and asking the question: who can fit better—is there someone more skilled?

If you take a look at the skills necessary for doing a job they might not necessarily be the same for building other people to do that job. Leadership is something that may evolve over a period of time and most people can learn certain skills. A person can learn to be a better listener, communicator, or to interact more effectively with others. If he or she is in that learning mode it will create an environment for change.

About John Moser

JOHN MOSER is a twenty-eight-year veteran of the professional training, development, speaking, and consulting world. He joined the world's largest international training organization as a sales associate in Washington, D.C., in 1978 following a career spanning six years as a professional golfer and member of the PGA. From 1980 to 1984 he was the number one salesperson worldwide and was then promoted to run the Leadership Institute of Washington, D.C., for eight years before forming his own training, coaching, consulting, and speaking organization.

Because of his vast experience and notoriety, John was invited to the White House in preparation for sending President Reagan to the Russian Summit. While in D.C. he was an annual trainer for the Defense Intelligence College and War College for twelve consecutive years.

Additionally, he was a former host of several live call-in radio shows including WERC *Street Talk* and WCEO *Monday Morning Sales Meeting*. He has appeared on a number of radio and television shows, including Fox, NBC, and various cable networks. He regularly has articles published in regional and national newspapers and magazines including *Smithsonian, Business to Business, Personal Selling Power,* and editions of the *Business Journal.*

Some additional clients include several beauty pageant winners including: the former Miss Alabama, Virginia, Maryland, and Miss America, six professional sports teams, IBM, ATT, Marriott, Cameron Valves, Parisians, O'Neal Steel, Merrill Lynch, First Protective, Oracle, Baptist Health Systems, NASA, FBI, Department of Agriculture, and Mercedes-Benz.

John Moser was born in Germany and attended college in Kentucky and Maryland.

John Moser
John Moser & Associates
823 Bishops Court
Birmingham, AL 35242

205.401.1303
jmoserbhm@aol.com
www.johnmoserspeaks.com

Chapter Six

An interview with...

Rubye Braye & Eric Evans

Autonomy: A Key Strategy for Success

David Wright (Wright)

Today we're talking with Rubye Braye and Eric Evans.

Rubye Braye, PD, is recognized as an authority in the field of leadership and organizational performance. The founder of Wu Li Turtle Corp., she is a trusted adviser, consultant, coach, and speaker on leadership and organizational performance for clients in both the public and private sectors. For more than twenty-five years her results-focused approach has guided leaders from organizations around the globe in reaching optimum performance levels. Among the clients Rubye has worked with are: American Friends Service Committee, Capella University, U.S. Defense Logistics Agency, Executive Security and Engineering Technologies, Fort Gordon, Morgan State University, Rwanda Yearly Meeting, Savannah State University, Tuskegee University, U.S. Defense Information Systems Agency, The Greenleaf Center for Servant Leadership, and Walden Institute. Prior to starting Wu Li Turtle, Rubye served more than twenty years as an active duty officer and was vice president for a technology firm in its southeastern regional office. In addition to her breadth of experience working with clients, she holds degrees in sociology and business administration from Hollins University, Boston University, and Walden University as well as leadership and executive coaching certificates from Harvard University and Georgetown University, respectively. Rubye is a peer reviewer for *The International Journal for Servant-Leadership* as well as a member of the American Management Association, American Society for Training and Development, Institute for Operations Research and Management Science, and the National Association of Female Executives.

Eric Evans is the founder and president of Peak Learning Companies, Inc. He is an alumnus of the University of North Carolina at Charlotte, with more than two decades facilitating corporate training programs and delivering inspirational keynote speaking engagements. He uses the wilderness as a metaphor and methodology for success in business and in life. He speaks from his own innovative model that illustrates how all people can accomplish any goal if they use five principle values illustrated in the F.I.V.E.-O. Model®. He works nationally and internationally coaching clients as they embrace new opportunities, develop innovative ideas, and learn new perspectives. His clients include a number of colleges and universities, Fortune 100 companies, professional sports league players, and spiritual leaders from developing countries. Whether he is in the classroom, boardroom, or an outdoor environment, he utilizes his unique background to promote positive change for all of the organizations he serves. He believes if you "inspire the heart, hands and feet will follow."® Eric is an avid outdoorsman who enjoys sharing rock and ice climbing, sea kayaking, and mountain biking. He currently lives in Minnesota with his lovely wife and two children.

Rubye and Eric, welcome to *Success Strategies!*

Rubye Braye (Braye)

Good morning, it's a pleasure to be with you, David!

Eric Evans (Evans)

Thank you, David!

Wright

So, what is "autonomy"?

Braye

Very simply put, the dictionary defines autonomy as independence or freedom. It's a way of being able to identify yourself in the world so that you have agency and can self-govern. In fact, it is a place of audacious power and boldness.

Wright

Do you have anything to add to that, Eric?

Evans

David, I agree with Rubye. Frankly, without autonomy I don't believe that you can control your own destiny. I believe it is a critical platform in creating success as well as commercial sustainability.

Wright

Why is autonomy so important?

Braye

Autonomy is really important because it allows you to accept responsibility for everything in your life. And when I say "everything," I'm talking about elevating your awareness so that you're in a position to consciously decide. You don't just give up your power to other people when there are things that are not working in your life. It gives you an opportunity to work on your mind, work on your body, and work to renew your spirit.

Now when I think about the mind for example, it's amazing how many things we are unaware of from day to day about ourselves. You cannot do better unless you can be better. You cannot be better without awareness. Autonomy is the basis for heightened awareness and action. "I am in charge, and I can act!" This attitude affects what we believe, and what we believe affects how we feel, and how we feel ultimately drives what we will do in the world.

Evans

Autonomy is very important in that it's the initial platform for institutional trust. You must be able to wisely control your direction throughout a marketplace. If you do not to a certain degree control your intellectual capital or the products that you develop, others will. And regaining control will be a challenge; so without autonomy you are at the whim of what others say you can and cannot do.

Wright

Why would a person want to be autonomous?

Braye

There are two very important reasons. First, when you think about success in the workplace, marketplace, and in the world, being autonomous if you are a leader puts you in a position much like Jim Collins (n.d.) described for Level Five leaders and having the right people. All are self-guided and motivated. Being self-motivated, one is often filled with ideas that are freely shared. These ideas help make organizations more productive.

Another reason someone would want to be autonomous is to be hired and set free. A company's board of directors or an employer can hire you and trust you. They can give you autonomy because you understand the purpose for the organization, and you will govern and lead in ways that will inspire others who are already motivated to use their ideas in ways that are oriented toward the purpose of the organization. If you head your own organization, being autonomous means that you don't need anybody driving you—you are self-driven, you are self-purposed, you are self-balanced, and you're self-organized. Being autonomous doesn't mean that you operate alone; it means that you have powerful bold conversations and work with others to be able to advance shared ideas. You have clarity around what must be done and you're motivated enough to get up and go do it.

Evans

Consider if you are working with two individuals or two commercial entities that come from a position of autonomy, they both have something to offer and they both are enriched because they both are coming from their own position of strength. I'm not operating in a sense because I absolutely need everything that the other person or company may have. They need what I have, and I need what they have. It's a win-win for both of us. We both can enter into an agreement to conduct business or develop relationships because we are both coming from positions of value and strength. We both have something to offer and we both have some confidence around controlling what we have to offer.

Wright

When one is autonomous, what are the possibilities?

Braye

The possibilities are almost infinite! There are possibilities for self. There are great possibilities in relationship with others. The individual is open to ideas and possibilities regarding the work. Increasingly important are the possibilities around stewardship of resources. These are resources that individuals and organizations internally have responsibility for, as well as those resources that we communally share. Let's take, for example, a person who understands autonomy related to self. This means that from day to day, this person is eating in ways that are healthy, and he or she is exercising and living a balanced life. Doing so models the way for others in an organization so that we don't have people who are stressed and working all the time.

I was reading an article the other day about Europeans who take thirty days of vacation every year. The average American struggles to take a week off at a time; many of them never do. Many take three-day vacations at a time, thinking that if they're away longer, they'll come back and the environment will be absolutely out of control. Autonomy, as a success strategy, provides a way of thinking that allows individuals who are leaders and individuals who are followers to trust and share control, being self-driven and self-motivated. Scheduling time away allows for rest and renewal, to support higher performance and greater productivity. There's a lovely story and a message from Hopi elders (n.d.). Some say that it was received in December of 1999. There are variations of the message, and this is one:

> "There is a river that is flowing now very fast, and it's so great and swift. There are those who will be afraid. They will try to hold onto the shore. They will feel they're being torn apart and will suffer greatly. Know that the river has its destination. The elders say that we must let go of the shore, push off into the middle of the river, keep our eyes open, and our heads above water. And I say, see who is in there with you and celebrate. At this time in history we are to take nothing personal, at least of all ourselves. So the moment that we do, our spiritual growth and journey comes to a halt. The time of the lone wolf is over. We must gather ourselves; we must banish the word 'struggle' from our attitude and vocabulary. All that we do not must be done in a sacred manner and in celebration. We are the ones we've been waiting for."

Do you think that is a message of autonomy? Absolutely. It is autonomy that says we're strong enough to decide to get out in the river. Together we can move forward. And in doing this together, each person has to be willing, self-motivated, and not afraid. It is not acceptable to simply be willing to stand on the side and watch or to wait for somebody else to lead. Each one of us can decide.

Evans

I agree 100 percent. When one is autonomous there is a level of confidence that is present. There is a level of courage that is inherent and where there is courage there is hope. I believe that hope is the catalyst for change and change is the tool for human success.

Wright

What must a person do to develop a sense of autonomy?

Braye

There are a number of things that a person may do to develop a sense of autonomy. The first is to simply decide, "I am going to be in charge of my life: my mind, my body, my relationships, my finances, my resources, and my work." And if we were to take them in order, we would first begin with the mind and body. The autonomous person says, "I will not be swayed by simply what is marketed to me by today's media. If it is not healthy and good for my mind and my body, I will shut it down and shut it out." That doesn't mean one is unaware of what is happening in the world—one just chooses to be a contrarian. And this is true for those in organizations as well as outside organizations. People who choose autonomy have a strong sense of what it takes to be healthy, mentally and physically, and they act from that place of knowing.

Next is to value people. People first. First always.

For an autonomous person, finances are important. Imagine that an autonomous person is somebody who has decided, "I will manage my finances, whether personal finances or organizational finances. I'll pay cash where possible. I'll stay out of debt. I will invest. I will own property as opposed to simply being a renter and debtor." These are strategies that are indicative of those who are autonomous and successful.

It also means that we will get rid of clutter—the things we don't need. I think about the storage unit business in America; it is such a growing industry; we can't build them fast enough. What that means is we are accumulating things we don't need and they sit in storage sheds. We do the same thing in our businesses. I think about the "just in time" delivery concept, where resources are purchased and used when needed. This frees space and eases cash flow for many companies that purchase when needed.

The last thing is to maintain personal balance and work/life harmony. Many of us are over engaged from day to day, with two to three jobs, trying to accumulate unneeded things. It is important to consciously decide, "This is something I will do because it is important for me, important for my organization." A real leader models the practice of autonomy in these ways as a success strategy.

Evans

I believe that in order to fully develop autonomy you must begin to build a sense of confidence, you must have courage, and you must take some risk. Many people are prevented from bringing their dreams into fruition because of fear. But the answer to being fearful is to be courageous. Courage means to me that one will assess a situation, evaluate the risk, and choose to move forward based on implementing the appropriate strategies that yield the desired outcome. You have to develop your skill set so you can be successful at whatever you choose. I'll give an example.

About fifteen years ago I pioneered an industry in the Southeastern part of the country. I opened up the first indoor rock-climbing gym in the State of North Carolina. I was a partner of the first one in South Carolina, and wrote the business plan for a number of other southern states. I did that based upon a number of reasons. One, I never believed that employers would pay you what you believe you're worth. I always believed employers would only pay you what that position is worth. I tend to think a lot of myself, and I tend to think that I am as worthy of as much money as I can get from the marketplace. I felt that the only way I could do this was to be autonomous and self-sustaining. I believed that I needed to be able to control my own destiny because of my concern that someone else may control it for me. I didn't want anyone to give me a minimum wage job. In fact, I remember once I was working for a company and the funniest thing happened, I served as the director of their program and the annual review came up. My boss ended up giving me a twenty-five-cent raise. I thought it was pretty laughable because at the same time we would have clients who would pay $25,000 for a one-day program. I thought, I'm responsible for people's lives and at best you will reward the position I hold with a mere twenty-five cents. At the same time, however, you would compensate yourself with as much of that $25,000 as you possibly could. That was when the light first dawned on for me about autonomy. Being autonomous is the only way you can control your own destiny, be it professional or personal. You have to be able, in my opinion, to drive the results that you want for your own personal values. I believe that when you ask what it takes to have that sense of autonomy, you must have some confidence, you must have courage, and you have to be willing to take risks—you've got to be the change that you're trying to make.

All of these things are what I embrace and that have allowed me to enjoy success in my own personal expression of life as I am today. And it's what I share with my clients and teach my children.

Wright

How are organizations and teams affected when individuals value autonomy?

Braye

Individuals and teams are affected in a number of ways when they value autonomy. They focus in ways that increase performance and productivity. When focus is clear it means that they have clear priorities and achieve both their business goals as well as their personal goals.

Just imagine what it is like in an organization when you have the kind of insight that allows you to share your knowledge and perspective in a way that is persuasive with those you hope will follow. When the information is communicated respectfully and purposefully, others may be motivated to act to achieve the goals. There is one caveat—there are times when we get so excited about the sharing that we will overwork, and so it's important to model work/life harmony. I referenced this earlier—an autonomous leader will always act as a governor, determining what a healthy culture in an organization should be like. The leader will determine whether or not there's trust so that ideas can be freely shared, as opposed to contained where individuals hold information close for job security. When individuals and their ideas are valued and openly recognized, they trust. They are not afraid that others will steal their ideas, take credit, and receive recognition. In this way, all win—individuals, teams, and the organization.

Wright

So what are the greatest workplace advantages of autonomy?

Braye

The greatest advantages are where the autonomous leader articulates then serves in a way that promotes a vision of success. It's amazing how many organizations fail simply because the leaders are so busy managing as opposed to leading. But when there's autonomy, a leader is clear about the vision and clear about the day-to-day mission and operations that must be oriented toward the vision. The leader has clarity regarding the goals, tasks, responsibilities, accountability, and what may be accomplished in a prioritized and "projectized" manner. There is a measure of success in the workplace when the vision is clearly articulated, so that each person understands the importance of their role.

This measure is further developed when each person's performance is consistent with the vision. The decision to contribute toward success is an outcome of autonomy, with workplace advantages for each individual, team, and the overall organization.

Evans

You know, I think additional workplace advantages of autonomy include the fact that you really get to move your entire team forward together because everybody is, for the most part, sharing a common goal, and everybody is negotiating and working from a place of strength. Everybody wins, and if it's not a win-win situation, people begin to consider other opportunities, in my opinion. They may or may not leave, but you will not get their full participation. They decide that "I need to look out for myself because I don't believe we collectively as a team are sharing the same goal, and if we're not sharing the same goal then we're not valued at the same level, so perhaps I need to look out for myself." And that's not what we all want. I believe from an autonomous perspective we all agree on where we want to go. We use strategies in order to get us from A to B and to determine what target we want to choose and how we effectively hit that target.

Wright

The title of this chapter is "Autonomy, the Ultimate Success Strategy." What makes it the ultimate success strategy?

Braye

Thinking about that question I'm reminded of a quote attributed to Michael Jordan. "Individuals win games, but teams win championships." An individual who's autonomous clearly understands what it's like to have a great game, but more importantly the player understands that in working with others as a team one can play in a way that *everybody* wins. Everybody's a champion. This means that the individual or the leader has self-mastery, a sense of independence, and freedom as well as trust and goodwill when it comes to interacting with others. This makes it possible to communicate persuasively and act as one for a powerful and a bold difference—the ultimate success strategy.

Wright

So, Eric, in your biographical sketch it mentions that you are the inventor of the F.I.V.E.-O® Model, is that correct?

Evans

That is absolutely correct.

Wright

Could you tell me what the F.I.V.E.-O® Model is?

Evans

It's actually an acronym, and I believe that every person on this planet can achieve anything in life if they receive and hold these five principle values. In fact, I offer this challenge: why do you do what you do? Why do I do what I do? All of us who walk the face of this earth have these values; that is why we do what we do.

In the F.I.V.E.-O Model acronym, the F stands for Faith, which is to believe in yourself, believe in your dreams and to believe in something larger than you. If you did not believe in something, you would not ever try to achieve it or make a difference.

The I stands for Identification. If I cannot identify with you I may not emulate your behavior. I don't want to be like you. Perhaps I can't even hear you.

The V is Value—either intrinsic value or financial value in something, because the combination of the two creates your value system. And you make decisions based upon what you value.

The E is Exposure—to know something exists. You can't choose green if you do not know it is a color. How could you say that you want to be a surgeon if you do not know there are doctors?

The O is Opportunity—to have a positive chance to try, believing that you continue to act in ways that result in success. And you quit doing things that you continually fail.

These five principles bring you to the crossroads of choices, and when you have choices you can make free decisions.

I work with people who stand at the crossroads. These people are executives, students, administrators, teachers—all of us—because at some point in our lives we all stand at that crossroad assessing our choices. To move forward, we all have to make decisions.

This model resulted from some of the earlier successes I had as a younger man. I started a number of businesses throughout the Southeast, and people wanted to base my success on my race or color—I'm a black guy, an African-American. I felt my success was the result of my skill set. It was based on what I believed in, the people and the things I identified with, and the values I embraced that allowed me to achieve. Frankly because I was exposed to a particular industry, I had a positive chance to participate. From that participation, I was able to leverage the experiences into business opportunities and speaking engagements where I now literally speak all around the country. I've spoken at Harvard Business School and numerous Fortune 100 companies, internationally, nationally, regionally, and all over on the topic of achievement. So I see it as a platform for all of us to begin to take that first leap to be able to develop that sense of trust; to be able to take those risks and to look for mentors and models that inspire us to take a step to move forward.

Wright

How does the F.I.V.E.-O Model play a role in your clients achieving success?

Evans

If you don't believe that you can be successful, you won't be. You won't even try. Sometimes some of us need examples of what success looks like. If you have not been exposed to successful outcomes, you might believe that there are no successful outcomes. And if you don't have opportunities, those newly learned skills and those developed characteristics remain unused; again simply put, you may not try. So I firmly believe that the way my clients use the F.I.V.E.-O Model as an achievement strategy is to allow the values it teaches to inspire them to dig deep, believe, and continue to change. The values inspire them to find the appropriate tools, and then wisely use those tools to create a more successful life achieving their particular goals.

Wright

Why is the F.I.V.E.-O Model important?

Evans

I believe it's critically important, David. Simply, we don't do things 100 percent that we don't believe in. We rarely continue to do things and work with people productively if we can't identify with them. If we don't share the same value system, we're on a different page—we're not evenly yoked. And again if I hadn't been exposed to successful outcomes I may not know what a successful outcome looks like. In our society the greatest tragedy is to be robbed of an opportunity to be successful. We continue to do things that we have success in, and we quit doing things that we continually fail at. The F.I.V.E.-O. Model is important in that it serves as a catalyst in helping one take the first step to action, which is to try. I believe "you should try to make a positive difference in any situation that you're in." You may not control the outcome, but the one thing you can control is how you respond. I believe you should be of assistance whenever you can.

I can identify with being in a situation where someone could possibly need help, and I would help because that's a value of mine. When I choose to act in a situation, it leaves me feeling very fortunate to have an opportunity to even try. Naturally at the end of the day, I know why the F.I.V.E.-O Model is important. I have in the past and still to this day believe that it is the stimulus to encourage one to take a step, to make one move forward, to make one *try* because if you try, at least you stand a chance of being successful. The only thing that is guaranteed not to bring success is to not try.

Wright

How has F.I.V.E.-O impacted your own personal successes?

Evans

It is the foundation for my existence. It is the reason I have enjoyed personal and professional success throughout my life. And it is part of the legacy I wish to leave with my children. I get so much joy from my children. I get joy from them because I see the opportunity to teach them to make a difference in this society that we live in.

The F.I.V.E.-O has impacted my own personal success in that it has allowed me to be self-employed. I've been self-employed now for more than twenty-two years—successfully self-employed. It has been important to me in that I'm able to use the F.I.V.E.-O as a guide to help friends, family, and clients with whom I work, inspiring them to do more, to reach down deep and approach life from a position of strength, courage, and confidence, and create opportunities that drive their own success.

I believe that when you come out of the womb you have everything in you that God gave you to accomplish anything that you put your mind to, but throughout life society tries to beat it out of you. By the time you're sixteen you no longer know what you want to do when you grow up. Then you're forty and you still don't know what you want to do when you grow up. Soon you're fifty and you're having a midlife crisis. Imagine if you could grow up and do what you wanted to do when you were young, innocent, and unencumbered by the expectations others put on you—before you were robbed of all of that inspiration and all of what God put inside of you to have a successful life. The F.I.V.E.-O Model has proven to be critically important for me in my entire walk on this journey we call life.

Wright

How does F.I.V.E.-O play a role in autonomy as a success strategy?

Evans

If I don't believe in what I'm doing, and if I don't believe in what you're doing, I can't work with you. I can't embrace your platform, because I simply don't believe in it. And when I say "embrace it," I mean whole-heartedly.

I have some clients who go to work every day and they *dread* their job—they dread it. They dread it because they don't necessarily agree with the platform from which they are operating. They don't share the same values of the folks they work with and it keeps them from putting 100 percent into their job. How does that play a role in productivity? How does that play a role in personal happiness?

I've always said people will only leave their job for three reasons. I call it the three P's. People leave their job because they no longer find or are satisfied with Personal growth, Professional development, or financial Prosperity. All of those things revolve around autonomy. When you have an autonomous person, he or she naturally internalizes the F.I.V.E.-O Model—the person has to believe. Autonomous people must identify, they must find value, and they have to be exposed to success. They must have a positive opportunity to be involved, so that's how I see how they compliment each other.

Wright

How does F.I.V.E.-O and autonomy allow your clients to thrive in the face of the ever-changing landscape of business and economy?

Evans

Simply because we all have to continue to look out at this landscape of industry and life, and the landscape itself keeps changing. This means you have to change. You have to continue to find things that you believe in, and you have to find clients who believe in you. You have to find and identify clients who need your product. You have to determine what the values of those clients are so you can see if there's a match. And then they have to have an opportunity to experience what you have to offer.

I believe that once you position yourself where you can benefit your client, you can continue to be successful in the changing landscape of commerce, economy and personal well-being.

Wright

Rubye, do you think that Faith, Identification, Value, Exposure, and Opportunity fit within your model of autonomy?

Braye

Absolutely! Unless you start with faith in yourself, it's a non-starter; there is no going forward. More and more leaders must have faith in the employees, value them and their contributions, and offer opportunities for development. Doing so will reduce the need to closely manage. Autonomy and accountability in the workforce foster quality regarding the work, the products, and the services. An example is in hospitals where the employees own the work and ensure safe healthcare conditions. Autonomy is important and the F.I.V.E.-O Model is an effective framework, for use in communicating it!

Wright

How do individuals as well as organizations benefit from a F.I.V.E.-O/autonomous success strategy?

Braye

I believe that individuals and organizations benefit in a significant way. If people decide to embrace autonomy where they're able to claim their own freedom, their own independence, their own power, their own boldness—where there's courage from day to day, where there is integrity from day to day—there is nothing that can happen in an organization that will shift them from that position.

When individuals choose to deviate from practices that are our finest and noblest, the result will be behaviors that are harmful for self, others, and harmful in the organizations where they serve. Therefore it's important to have a really strong clear sense of one's personhood, of agency, of how one will choose to govern self. And when that's clear, one can choose to lead an organization in that way and have a culture where people are not covering themselves all the time, where there's freedom and openness regarding sharing ideas, where people are able to live balanced wholesome, healthy lives, both in the workplace as well how they choose to live in their families.

That reminds me of a concept I remember writing about years ago that had to do with having a personal life and a professional life. The very idea implies duplicity, and I don't believe it is possible. I believe that each of us has a life. In life, we serve portions of our time in various roles. We have roles with family members as daughters, mothers, sisters, fathers, brothers as well as employees and leaders in organizations.

Our values serve as the basis for how we will choose to behave in all of these roles. Autonomy gives us an opportunity from a self-governing perspective to place the bar really high, which makes decision-making easy. And when people in our families and in the workplace hear stories that are inconsistent with the person they know us to be, they can say, "Oh no, I know this person. There's no way that's true!" The F.I.V.E.-O Model helps to guide our life practice in this way.

Wright

How does F.I.V.E.-O create lasting and measurable change in your individual clients, and in organizations?

Evans

I believe that it is lasting because it gives my clients a template to identify opportunity.

I have significant experiences in outdoor adventure, and I use the wilderness as a methodology to create a mirror for self-reflection. I believe the way a person reacts in an artificial environment is the same way they act in a real environment, so I may take you out on a trip with me and we may go on a climbing trip or a kayaking trip or just a basic hike. We are going to encounter certain hurdles along our journey. The way that you react in that environment is going to be the same as how you react in your natural environment. If you are faced with adversity, and you have a miserable time out in the wilderness with me, it is likely that you are going to be hesitant to go back out with me again. The same thing will happen with you in your job or professional environment. If you go to your job and you're having an absolute miserable time, you're not enjoying it, and you no longer share the same values with the folks you're working with, you may begin to look toward leaving that job. This is one way leaders are able to measure whether change takes place. If the change is negative, they'll be able to measure that change by the exiting of employees.

One of the things that I'm pretty big on is what I call the five R's. They are: Recruiting, Retaining, Retraining, Retailing, and the Relationships between your people and your products and services. I believe that a team that's been together for quite some time can be very effective. A well-oiled machine can be the most efficient machine. One of the key platforms in my mind for keeping that machine together is keeping the machine inspired. I use the F.I.V.E.-O Model as a way to revisit the answers to key questions: "Do we still believe in what we're doing? Are we all on board? Do we still identify with the common goal? Do we still see the value? Are we still having a positive experience, having fun, and accomplishing the goals that we set our minds on?" I believe that at the end of the day you're able to measure this by conducting a social litmus test. Check in with your team, and based on whether you're reaching the desired targets or goals, their feedback becomes the barometer that determines the necessity of changing your course of strategy.

Braye

Lasting change is possible when a practice is future oriented, positive, and self-initiated. In these ways, our autonomous practice becomes maintainable. Will we decide on our own to live autonomously? If so, this precious, fine, noble quality will show up in how we choose to be, what we choose to do, and what we choose to say—with no equivocation. This is the ultimate success strategy.

Wright

This has been a great conversation! I really appreciate both of you and your input into this very important chapter.

Collins, J. (n.d.). "Getting the right people on the bus—and the wrong people off the bus—in a family business." Retrieved November 5, 2007, from http://www.jimcollins.com/hall/index.html.

Hopi elders' message (n.d.). Retrieved November 5, 2007, from http://www.mayanmajix.com/art034.html.

About Rubye Braye & Eric Evans

RUBYE BRAYE, PH.D., Wu Li Turtle Corp., is a trusted adviser, consultant, coach, and speaker on leadership and organizational performance for clients in both the public and private sectors. She has guided organizational leaders in reaching optimum performance levels. She served more than twenty years as an active duty officer and was a vice president for a technology firm in its southeastern regional office. She holds degrees in sociology and business administration from Hollins University, Boston University, and Walden University as well as leadership and executive coaching certificates from Harvard University and Georgetown University, respectively.

ERIC EVANS is the founder and president of Peak Learning Companies Inc. He is an alumnus of the University of North Carolina at Charlotte, with more than two decades facilitating corporate training programs and delivering inspirational keynote speaking engagements. He uses the wilderness as a metaphor and methodology for success in business and in life. He speaks from his own innovative model that illustrates how all people can accomplish any goal if they use five principle values illustrated in the F.I.V.E.-O Model®. He works nationally and internationally coaching clients as they embrace new opportunities, develop innovative ideas, and learn new perspectives. His clients include a number of colleges and universities, Fortune 100 companies, professional sports league players, and spiritual leaders from developing countries. Whether he is in the classroom, boardroom, or an outdoor environment, he utilizes his unique background to promote positive change for all of the organizations he serves. He believes if you "inspire the heart, hands and feet will follow."®

Rubye Braye
Wu Li Turtle Corp.
Phone: 703.864.3769
E-mail: e@wuliturtle.com
www.wuliturtle.con

Eric L. Evans
Peak Learning Companies Inc.
Phone: 651.338.0976
E-mail: Peaklearnig@comcast.net
www.peaklearningco.com

Chapter Seven

An interview with...

Jerry Hogan

The Power of Procrastination

David Wright (Wright)

After graduating from the United States Naval Academy, Jerry Hogan served as a Marine officer for six years. Following his military service, he spent twenty-seven years helping companies grow and prosper through increased sales, decreased expenses, and people development.

In 2000, Jerry founded *The Resource Development Group LLC,* with the vision of "Changing the World, one Attitude at a Time." The organizational development processes he facilitates in leadership, sales, and strategic planning have been instrumental in changing the lives and fortunes of thousands of people, and have earned him recognition from several national and regional leadership development organizations.

The title of this chapter is "The Power of Procrastination." How did you come up with this name?

Jerry Hogan (Hogan)

In my years both in business for others and for myself I came to the realization that many people who got very good results in their work seemed to be people who put things off to the last minute. I never really understood that until I was mentored by one of my heroes in the business, Doug Brown. He explained to me the concept of *possibility thinking* and *necessity thinking*. When I was able to understand that a good many people are *necessity thinkers,* I could see how many of us are built so that we work best under pressure.

I have been privileged to meet a number of Congressional Medal of Honor winners and I have read many of their biographies. Not one single Congressional Medal of Honor winner has ever been awarded the medal for good planning! These men did what was necessary, under the most dire conditions—when it was necessary.

People in many circumstances tend to function at their highest level when under the highest pressure. Deadlines will very often provide that kind of pressure, getting the adrenalin pumping and getting people to work at their best. I thought if there is a way to tap into that natural phenomenon of *necessity thinking,* perhaps everyone would have a way to improve their lives and get greater success in all they do.

Wright

What is *necessity thinking*?

Hogan

Necessity thinking is better explained in terms of *necessity thinker* verses *possibility thinker.*

A *possibility thinker* is somebody who is able to plan long-term and take action on his or her plans long-term because the possibility thinker is primarily motivated by reward.

A *necessity thinker* is someone who is motivated primarily by the avoidance of failure or pain. The tasks that these people perform are more likely to be those that will keep them out of trouble as opposed to giving them the rewards they are looking for.

Wright

Doesn't this fly in the face of conventional wisdom about success?

Hogan

I think it does, in a way. Thousands of books about success and motivation have been written over the years and virtually all of them are very good and have great material. I ask myself why is it that if these books are so good, if the material is so important, and so logical, why do so many people not succeed at the level of their dreams? What I came to realize is that most of the books are written for *possibility thinkers.* They are written for people who dream big and who have the ability to plan over a long period of time to methodically do those things that are necessary to get what they want.

Necessity thinkers also have the ability to dream big, but unlike *possibility thinkers,* who are motivated primarily by rewards, necessity thinkers are more motivated by avoidance of pain or consequences for inaction.

So yes, it does fly in the face of conventional thinking. It also taps into the heart and soul of why so many people fail. For one reason or another, they are unable to think like a *possibility thinker* and act that way.

Wright

Are you saying that people should put off doing important tasks?

Hogan

Not at all. What I'm saying is that people should do important tasks when they are psychologically and physically at their peak to do them. That is usually when a deadline approaches or when a situation that is deemed an emergency occurs. The activity focus becomes very targeted and the actions are directed toward the accomplishment of clear specific purpose.

Wright

What about planning? Is it important?

Hogan

Of course it's important. If you're a *necessity thinker* and you are motivated by the consequences of not succeeding or by emerging deadlines, what you've got to understand is that planning needs to begin with a view toward the end. Start planning for that very last day when something is due, and then plan backward so that each intermediate goal is reached in time to begin the next step toward the final, large goal.

Let's say we have a project or a task that needs to be done in two weeks. We know that with concerted effort, the work will only take about two hours to accomplish. A good *necessity thinking* planner would plan to begin that job on the day of or the day before it is due. However, since we have been trained in *possibility thinking,* we typically feel guilty about procrastinating for thirteen days until we actually get it started. It is just reverse planning. Begin with the end in mind; only this time, the end is the due date as well as the actual completion of the task.

Wright

Aren't all high achievers possibility thinkers?

Hogan

No, not at all. Let's go back to the Medal of Honor winners. Every one of those people found themselves in a *necessity thinking* environment in which a dire emergency or a high stress environment was encountered. They all performed at an extraordinary level. Throughout history we see examples of *necessity thinkers* who have preformed at higher levels than they ever preformed in a *possibility* environment. Harry S. Truman, as President of the United States is a good example of this. When Harry was a haberdasher, a Senator, and Vice President he had a fairly unremarkable career. Then upon assuming the Presidency he was put into a role in which he had to perform or the nation would die. Harry rose to that occasion and we won World War II as a result.

Wright

How do people know if they are *possibility thinkers* or *necessity thinkers?*

Hogan

I think it is easy to tell. You are probably a *necessity thinker* if you tend to put off until tomorrow what you think you should be doing today, but you are still getting it accomplished in a time frame that meets the deadline. What motivates you: the reward of accomplishment or the pain of not accomplishing something?

If you're a *possibility thinker* you are motivated by rewards. If you are a *necessity thinker* you're motivated by avoiding failure.

Wright

Is it possible to be a mixture?

Hogan

I think that it is. What typically occurs is that people are conditioned to be *necessity thinkers.* Many children behave because they didn't want to be spanked in the days of spanking. Children don't want to receive punishment. So consequently they establish the habits of *necessity thinking*. They may have the capability of being *possibility thinkers.* They may be accomplishing a great many things outside of a particular environment that requires them to be *necessity thinkers.*

If you can tap into your hidden resources of *possibility thinking* and apply *necessity thinking* to those activities, you can accomplish a great deal in a small amount of time.

Wright

If I'm a *necessity thinker*. How can I apply this characteristic to achieve my dreams, or avoid the consequences of inaction?

Hogan

First, recognize the fact that you are a *necessity thinker,* which is not a bad thing. It's who you are.

Secondly, ask yourself what has been stopping you to this point from achieving all that you dream of. If it is inaction, then ask yourself what will motivate you to achieve both important and urgent actions, *and what are the consequences for inaction?*

Establish some real life deadlines in which you will have a great deal of pain if you miss those deadlines. Occasionally you will miss one; we all miss deadlines. If the pain is real, the motivation to act is real. If you are a *necessity thinker,* choose those things that will cause you to act to avoid consequences that are as dire as the level of reward that you want to achieve. If you are want to accomplish something big and you don't accomplish it, make sure the penalties of not accomplishing it are as big as the rewards for accomplishing it.

Start planning from the back. Start planning from the day when whatever you want to accomplish is due, then work back from that day. When you begin a task, give yourself just enough time or a little bit more to accomplish what it is you are trying to accomplish. That will get your adrenalin running; it will focus the activities and will bring you to a high level of achievement.

Wright

If a person is a necessity thinker, can they ever become possibility thinkers?

Hogan

Sure they can. In my business we have an equation or a cycle of success. Results are driven by behaviors and behaviors are driven by attitudes. We achieve as a direct result of what we do. What we do is driven by how we feel. It is a circular equation. Attitudes drive behaviors and behaviors drive results that then drive attitudes. As we achieve more and more by applying the concept of *necessity thinking,* ironically our thinking becomes more oriented toward positive results and rewards. We will find ourselves more and more of a *possibility thinker.*

Wright

Are you a *possibility thinker* or a *necessity thinker,* and how do you use this characteristic?

Hogan

Let's say I'm becoming more of a *possibility thinker.* I belong to a network of about eight hundred organizational development specialists and we meet on a quarterly basis for training, motivation, and friendship. At these quarterly training sessions we're recognized for different levels of achievement. Each quarter I set a goal for what level of achievement I'm going to receive or be recognized for at the next quarterly training session. I tell a trusted friend to hold me accountable, so that when I show up at the quarterly, if I have not achieved that level of success, I don't receive the recognition that I had planned to achieve. To me that is a very disappointing thing. I also know that someone else knows.

That has kept me in very good stead over many years. Virtually every quarter I achieve some level of recognition for my results for the previous quarter.

This ties into another aspect of *necessity thinking—necessity thinkers* are short-term planners verses long-term planners. I have a very hard time looking out a year or two or five, but I can comfortably work in an environment of eight to twelve weeks. I set smaller goals that I can achieve in a shorter period of time and I watch the goals build upon each other to eventually get the higher goals that I'm looking to achieve.

Wright

I used to hate those seminars where I would be asked where I want to be five years from today. I would think that I don't even remember what I ate for lunch yesterday. This is hard for me.

Hogan

So this concept rings true for you.

Wright

That's right. So how do you proactively use the characteristic of your thinking model?

Hogan

The first thing is that just like *possibility thinkers, necessity thinkers* are able to dream. We have that capability. We know what we would like to achieve. The disconnect comes in putting together the concrete plan.

What I do is I decide what it is I'm going to go after—what it is I am going to achieve. Then I break that into small chunks of short-terms goals. I make those goals as short-term as I possibly can and I commit them not just to myself but to someone else as well. Then every day I review that goal in my morning meditation and I unconsciously drive myself toward taking actions via the process of internalization in the morning.

I find myself working toward specific small goals on a short-term basis. For instance, we just finished a major remodeling project in our house. I figured out how much money it was going to be and then I decided through a goal planning process how much money I needed to earn on a monthly basis. My goal was that much every month.

When I got within a healthy percentage of having that money available for the remodeling I went ahead and contracted for the remodeling. The fact that I contracted and that we had a start date for the process drove me to find enough more clients so that when the process of remodeling started I would have enough money to pay for it. It was that last bit where I actually made the contract that forced me to take the action necessary to earn the money to pay for the remodeling job.

Wright

I'm going to turn this over in my mind. I've never heard about the power of procrastination before. If it is okay with you I'll tell my wife that you gave me the right to be a procrastinator and I don't have to do all those things she wants me to do.

Hogan

Maybe the title is a bit misleading. It only appears to be procrastinating. When you were in eighth grade, you had to read *Huckleberry Finn.* Your English teacher probably gave you that book during the first day of class and said that the book report would be due on the last day of class before break. How many kids in that class started reading that book that night?

Wright

None of the kids I knew.

Hogan

There is always one girl who does—the curve breaker! The vast majority of students wait until a short time before that report is due. They read it, they cram information into their brains, they write the book report, and for the most part they get decent grades.

If you had planned to do it that way you wouldn't have to be spending all of those weeks and months, worrying about getting it done and listening to your conscience or your teacher or your parents complaining about your not getting it done. The plan was there and you are comfortable that you've given yourself enough time to do it. It is not really procrastination—it is really just forward planning.

Wright

Jerry, I appreciate the time you have spent with me today. It has been fascinating. I have recognized myself at times as a *necessity thinker* and I have also recognized myself as a *possibility thinker.* I may want to develop some measurements where I can use either one or both of them. In any event, I really appreciate the information and I think this is going to be great reading in our book.

Hogan

I appreciate the opportunity to talk with you about it and for hanging in, even with a topic that seems a little strange.

Wright

Jerry, thank you for being with us today on *Success Strategies.*

Hogan

Thank you, David.

About Jerry Hogan

After graduating from the United States Naval Academy, Jerry became an officer in the U.S. Marine Corps, serving as a combat commander during the evacuation of Saigon, as an artillery battery Executive Officer, and as Executive Officer of Marine recruiters for Michigan and Indiana. After six years, he transferred to the Reserves and served an additional four years as a Captain.

Upon leaving the Marine Corps, Jerry joined Corning Glass Works as a production supervisor. In eighteen months he had increased his department's efficiency by 62 percent and was promoted to Customer Service Manager for Electronic Products. For two consecutive years, his organization received "Vendor of the Year" awards from the world's largest electronics company. Jerry was promoted to Project Manager to direct the logistics and marketing of a manufacturing transfer from Pennsylvania to Taiwan.

Jerry continued his business growth with significant sales and profitability increases as Director of Sales Development, Director of Global Accounts, VP of Sales, and VP Sales and Marketing at various electronics and medical products firms for more than twenty years. As area manager for the United States Chamber of Commerce, he received the top award for membership growth. He has a great deal of experience in international markets, and has traveled extensively throughout four continents, both as a supplier and procurer of products.

As president of The Resource Development Group LLC, Jerry has expanded the company throughout Indiana and has been recognized as a leader in organizational development by two of the nation's leading training and development companies. Jerry was "Member of the Year" and president of Lake City Business Network International.

Jerry now shares the experience and knowledge he gained in more than thirty years as a successful executive. While teaching the principles of human resources development, strategic planning, and world-class manufacturing principles, Jerry has significantly contributed to the personal and organizational success of many companies and organizations. The processes he facilitates have been proven effective in enhancing the performance of people and operations, in building teamwork, and in improving the lives of the individual participants. In addition, an organization's bottom line is enhanced greatly when people are performing at their peaks and processes are aligned with the objectives of the company.

Jerry Hogan
The Resource Development Group LLC
2814 Patterson Road
Warsaw, IN 46582

574.551.7400
jerry@resourcedevelopmentgroup.com
www.resourcedevelopmentgroup.com

Chapter Eight

An interview with...

Brian Tracy

Some Timeless Truths & Principles of Success

David Wright (Wright)

Many years ago, Brian Tracy started off on a lifelong search for the secrets of success in life and business. He studied, researched, traveled, worked, and taught for more than thirty years. In 1981, he began to share his discoveries in talks and seminars, and eventually in books, audios, and video-based courses.

The greatest secret of success he learned is this: "There are no secrets of success." There are instead timeless truths and principles that have to be rediscovered, relearned, and practiced by each person. Brian's gift is synthesis—the ability to take large numbers of ideas from many sources and combine them into highly practical, enjoyable, and immediately usable forms that people can take and apply quickly to improve their life and work. Brian has brought together the best ideas, methods, and techniques from thousands of books, hundreds of courses, and experience working with individuals and organizations of every kind in the United States, Canada, and worldwide.

Today, I have asked Brian to discuss his book, *Victory! : Applying the Military Principals of Strategy for Success in Business and Personal Life*. (By the way it is refreshing to hear someone say something good about the successes of the military.)

Brian, why do you think the military is so successful?

Tracy

Well, the military is based on very serious thought. The American military is the most respected institution in America. Unless you're a left liberal, limp-wristed pinko, most people in America really respect the military because it keeps America free. People who join the military give up most of their lives—twenty to thirty years—in sacrifice to be prepared to guard our freedoms. And if you ask around the world what it is that America stands for, it stands for individual freedom, liberty, democracy, freedom, and the kind of opportunity that is only secured in a challenging world—a dangerous world—by your military.

Now the other thing is that the people in our military are not perfect because there is no human institution made up of human beings that is perfect—there are no perfect people. The cost of mistakes in military terms is death; therefore, people in the military are extraordinarily serious about what they do. They are constantly looking for ways to do what they do better and better and better to reduce the likelihood of losing a single person.

We in America place extraordinary value on individual human life. That is why you will see millions of dollars spent to save a life, whether for an accident victim or Siamese twins from South America, because that's part of our culture. The military has that same culture.

I was just reading today about the RQ-1 "Predator" drone planes (Unmanned Aerial Vehicles—UAVs) that have been used in reconnaissance over the no-fly zones in Iraq. These planes fly back and forth constantly gathering information from the ground. They can also carry remote-controlled weapons. According to www.globalsecurity.org, the planes cost $4.5 million each and get shot down on a regular basis. However, the military is willing to invest hundreds of millions of dollars to develop these planes, and lose them to save the life of a pilot because pilots are so precious—human life is precious.

In the military everything is calculated right down to the tinniest detail because the smallest details can cost lives. That is why the military is so successful—they are so meticulous about planning.

A salesperson can go out and make a call; if it doesn't work that's fine—he or she can make another sales call. Professional soldiers can go out on an operation and if it's not successful they're dead and maybe everybody in the squad is dead as well. There is no margin for error in the military; that's why they do it so well. This is also why the military principals of strategy that I talk about in *Victory*! are so incredibly important. A person who really understands those principals and strategies sees how to do things vastly better with far lower probability of failure than the average person.

Wright

In the promotion on *Victory*! You affirm that it is very important to set clear attainable goals and objectives. Does that theme carry out through all of your presentations and all of your books?

Tracy

Yes. Over and over again the theme reiterates that you can't hit a target you can't see. You shouldn't get into your car unless you know where you are going. More people spend more time planning a picnic than they spend planning their careers.

I'll give you an example. A very successful woman (she is in her fifties at the time of this interview) wrote down a plan when she was attending university. Her plan was for the first ten years she would work for a Fortune 500 corporation—really learn the business and learn how to function at high levels. For the second ten years of her career she talked about getting married and having children at the same time. For that second ten years she would also work for a medium sized company helping it grow and succeed. For the third ten years (between the ages of forty and fifty), she would start her own company based on her knowledge of both businesses. She would then build that into a successful company. Her last ten years she would be chief executive officer of a major corporation and retire financially independent at the age of sixty. At age fifty-eight she would have hit every single target. People would say, "Boy, you sure are lucky." No, it wouldn't be luck. From the time she was seventeen she was absolutely crystal clear about what she was going to do with her career and what she was going to do with her life, and she hit all of her targets.

Wright

In a time where companies, both large and small, take a look at their competition and basically try to copy everything they do, it was really interesting to read in *Victory*! that you suggest taking vigorous offensive action to get the best results. What do you mean by "vigorous offensive action"?

Tracy

Well, see, that's another thing. When you come back to talking about probabilities—and this is really important—you see successful people try more things. And if you wanted to just end the interview right now and ask, "What piece of advice would you give to our listeners?" I would say, "Try more things." The reason I would say that is because if you try more things, the probability is that you will hit your target

For example, here's an analogy I use. Imagine that you go into a room and there is a dartboard against the far wall. Now imagine that you are drunk and you have never played darts before. The room is not very bright and you can barely see the bull's eye. You are standing along way from the board, but you have an endless supply of darts. You pick up the darts and you just keep throwing them at the target over there on the other of the room even though you are not a good dart thrower and you're not even well coordinated. If you kept throwing darts over and over again what would you eventually hit?

Wright

Pretty soon you would get a bull's eye.

Tracy

Yes, eventually you would hit a bull's eye. The odds are that as you keep throwing the darts even though you are not that well educated, even if you don't come from a wealthy family or you don't have a Harvard education, if you just keep throwing darts you will get a little better each time you throw. It's known as a "decybernetic self-correction mechanism" in the brain—each time you try something, you get a little bit smarter at it. So over time, if you kept throwing, you must eventually hit a bull's eye. In other words, you must eventually find the right way to do the things you need to do to become a millionaire. That's the secret of success. That's why people come here from a 190 countries with one idea in mind—"If I come here I can try anything I want; I can go anywhere, because there are no limitations. I have so much freedom; and if I keep doing this, then by God, I will eventually hit a bull's eye." And they do and everybody says, "Boy, you sure where lucky."

Now imagine another scenario: You are thoroughly trained at throwing darts—you have practiced, you have developed skills and expertise in your field, you are constantly upgrading your knowledge, and you practice all the time. Second you are completely prepared, you're thoroughly cold sober, fresh, fit, alert, with high energy. Third, all of the room is very bright around the dartboard. This time how long would it take you to hit the bull's eye? The obvious answer is you will hit a bull's eye far faster than if you had all those negative conditions.

What I am I saying is, you can dramatically increase the speed at which you hit your bull's eye. The first person I described—drunk, unprepared, in a darkened room, and so on—may take twenty or twenty-five years. But if you are thoroughly prepared, constantly upgrading your skills; if you are very clear about your targets; if you have everything you need at hand and your target is clear, your chances of hitting a bull's eye you could hit a bull's eye is five years rather than twenty. That's the difference in success in life.

Wright

In reading your books and watching your presentations on video, one of the common threads seen through your presentations is creativity. I was glad that in the promotional material of *Victory*! you state that you need to apply innovative solutions to overcome obstacles. The word "innovative" grabbed me. I guess you are really concerned with *how* people solve problems rather than just solving problems.

Tracy

Vigorous action means you will cover more ground. What I say to people, especially in business, is the more things you do the more experience you get. The more experience you get the smarter you get. The smarter you get the better results you get the better results you get. The better results you get the less time it takes you to get the same results. And it's such a simple thing. In my books *Create Your Own Future* and *Victory*! you will find there is one characteristic of all successful people—they are action oriented. They move fast, they move quickly, and they don't waste time. They're moving ahead, trying more things, but they are always in motion. The faster you move the more energy you have. The faster you move the more in control you feel and the faster you are the more positive and the more motivated you are. We are talking about a direct relationship between vigorous action and success.

Wright

Well, the military certainly is a team "sport" and you talk about building peak performance teams for maximum results. My question is how do individuals in corporations build peak performance teams in this culture?

Tracy

One of the things we teach is the importance of selecting people carefully. Really successful companies spend an enormous amount of time at the front end on selection they look for people who are really, really good in terms of what they are looking for. They interview very carefully; they interview several people and they interview them several times. They do careful background checks. They are as careful in selecting people as a person might be in getting married. Again, in the military, before a person is promoted they go through a rigorous process. In large corporations, before a person is promoted his or her performance is very, very carefully evaluated to be sure they are the right people to be promoted at that time.

Wright

My favorite point in *Victory*! is when you say, "Amaze your competitors with surprise and speed." I have done that several times in business and it does work like a charm.

Tracy

Yes, it does. Again one of the things we teach over and over again that there is a direct relationship between speed and perceived value. When you do things fast for people they consider you to be better. They consider your products to be better and they consider your service to be better—they actually consider them to be of higher value. Therefore, if you do things really, really fast then you overcome an enormous amount of resistance. People wonder, "Is this a good decision? Is it worth the money?

Am I going the right direction?" When you do things fast, you blast that out of their minds.

Wright

You talk about moving quickly to seize opportunities. I have found that to be difficult. When I ask people about opportunities, it's difficult to find out what they think an opportunity is. Many think opportunities are high-risk, although I've never found it that way myself. What do you mean by moving quickly to cease opportunity?

Tracy

There are many cases were a person has an idea and they think that's a good idea. They think they should do something about it. They think, "I am going to do something about that but I really can't do it this week, so I will wait until after the month ends," and so on. By the time they do move on the opportunity it's to late—somebody's already seized it.

One of the military examples I use is the battle of Gettysburg. Now the battle of Gettysburg was considered the high-water mark of the Confederacy after the battle of Gettysburg the Confederacy won additional battles at Chattanooga and other places but they eventually lost the war. The high-water mark of Gettysburg was a little hill at one end of the battlefield called Little Round Top. As the battle began Little Round Top was empty. Colonel Joshua Chamberlain of the Union Army saw that this could be the pivotal point of the battlefield. He went up there and looked at it and he immediately rushed troops to fortify the hill. Meanwhile, the Confederates also saw that Little Round Top could be key to the battle as well, so they too immediately rushed the hill. An enormous battle took place. It was really the essence of the battle of Gettysburg. The victor who took that height controlled the battlefield. Eventually the union troops, who were almost lost, controlled Little Round Top and won the battle. The Civil War was over in about a year and a half, but that was the turning point.

So what would have happened if Chamberlain had said, "Wait until after lunch and then I'll move some men up to Little Round Top"? The Confederate troops would have seized Little Round Top, controlled the battlefield, and would have won the battle of Gettysburg. It was just a matter of moving very, very fast. Forty years later it was determined that there were three days at the battle of Gettysburg that cost the battle for the Confederates. The general in charge of the troops on the Confederate right flank was General James Longstreet. Lee told him to move his army forward as quickly as possible the next day, but to use his own judgment. Longstreet didn't agree with Lee's plan so he kept his troop sitting there most of the next day. It is said that it was Longstreet's failure to move forward on the second day and seize Little Round Top that cost the Confederacy the battle and eventually the war. It was just this failure to move forward and forty years later, when Longstreet appeared at a reunion of Confederate veterans in 1901 or 1904, he was booed. The veterans felt his failure to move forward that fateful day cost them the war. If you read every single account of the battle of Gettysburg, Longstreet's failure to move forward and quickly seize the opportunity is always included.

Wright

In your book you tell your readers to get the ideas and information needed to succeed. Where can individuals get these ideas?

Tracy

Well we are living in an ocean of ideas. It's so easy. The very first thing you do is you pick a subject you want to major in and you go to someone who is good at it. You ask what you should read in this field and you go down to the bookstore and you look at the books. Any book that is published in paperback obviously sold well in hardcover. Read the table of contents. Make sure the writer has experience in the area you in which you want to learn about. Buy the book and read it. People ask, "How can I be sure it is the right book?" You can't be sure; stop trying to be sure.

When I go to the bookstore I buy three or four books and bring them home and read them. I may only find one chapter of a book that's helpful, but that chapter may save me a year of hard work.

The fact is that your life is precious. A book costs twenty of thirty dollars. How much is your life worth? How much do you earn per hour? A person who earns fifty thousand dollars a year earns twenty-five dollars an hour. A person who wants to earn a hundred thousand dollars a year earns fifty dollars an hour. Now, if a book cost you ten or twenty dollars but it can save you a year of hard work, then that's the cheapest thing you have bought in your whole life. And what if you bought fifty books and you paid twenty dollars apiece for them—a thousand dollars worth of books—and out of that you only got one idea that saved you a year of hard work? You've got a fifty times payoff. So the rule is you cannot prepare too thoroughly.

Wright

In the last several months I have recommended your book, *Get Paid More and Promoted Faster* to more people. I have had a lot of friends in their fifties and sixties who have lost their jobs to layoffs all kinds of transfers of ownership. When I talked with you last, the current economy had a 65 percent jump in layoffs. In the last few months before I talked with you, every one of them reported that the book really did help them. They saw some things a little bit clearer; it was a great book.

How do you turn setbacks and difficulties to your advantage? I know what it means, but what's the process?

Tracy

You look into it you look into every setback and problem and find the seed of an equal or greater advantage or benefit. It's a basic rule. You find that all successful people look into their problems for lessons they can learn and for things they can turn to their advantage. In fact, one of the best attitudes you can possibly have is to say that you know every problem that is sent to you is sent to help you. So your job is just simply look into to it and ask, "What can help me in this situation?" And surprise, surprise! You will find something that can help you. You will find lessons you can learn; you will find something you can do more of, or less of; you can find something that will give you an insight that will set you in a different direction, and so on.

Wright

I am curious. I know you have written a lot in the past and you are a terrific writer. Your cassette programs are wonderful. What do you have planned for the next few years?

Tracy

Aside from speaking and consulting with non-profits, my goal is to produce four books a year on four different subjects, all of which have practical application to help people become more successful.

Wright

Well, I really want to thank you for your time here today. It's always fascinating to hear what you have to say. I know I have been a Brian Tracy fan for many, many years. I really appreciate your being with us today.

Tracy

Thank you. You have a wonderful day and I hope our listeners and readers will go out and get *Focal Point* and/or *Victory*! They are available at any bookstore or at Amazon.com. They are fabulous books, filled with good ideas that will save you years of hard work.

Wright

I have already figured out that those last two books are a better buy with Amazon.com, so you should go to your computer and buy these books as soon as possible.

We have been talking today with Brian Tracy, whose life and career truly makes one of the best rags-to-riches stories. Brian didn't graduate from high school and his first job was washing dishes. He lost job after job—washing cars, pumping gas, stacking lumber, you name it. He was homeless and living in his car. Finally, he got into sales, then sales management. Later, he sold investments, developed real estate, imported and distributed Japanese automobiles, and got a master's degree in business administration. Ultimately, he became the COO of a $265 million dollar development company.

Brian, you are quite a person. Thank you so much for being with us today.

Tracy

You are very welcome, David. You have a great day!

About Brian Tracy

One of the world's top success motivational speakers, Brian Tracy is the author of may books and audio tape seminars, including The Psychology of Achievement, The Luck Factor, Breaking the Success Barrier, Thinking Big and Success Is a Journey.

Brian Tracy
www.BrianTracy.com

Chapter Nine

An interview with...

Diane Amundson

Humility Leads the Way

David Wright (Wright)

Today we are talking with Diane Amundson. She is the founder and the CEO of Diane Amundson and Associates. As an organizational consultant and trainer for the past fifteen years, she has observed how companies are being led, and in particular, the characteristics of their leaders. Much has been written about the need for leaders to be visionary, good communicators, and risk-takers. She believes that while these characteristics are vital, she has concluded that upstream of these attributes is a foundation of humility that must be present before a leader will have effective followers. When a leader is clear about his or her strengths and areas of weaknesses, the leader is able to seek out complementing strengths in others, and to listen to the opposing viewpoints that will help the leader's organization grow.

Diane, welcome to *Success Strategies*.

Diane Amundson (Amundson)

Thank you, David.

Wright

Why are we talking about humility in relation to leadership?

Amundson

As a consultant for over fifteen years, I have worked with hundreds of small, medium, and large organizations, and while working with them, my curiosity led me to observe the role of the leader and what makes him or her effective. In my observations, I discovered a common thread of humility or vulnerability in the effective leaders. These leaders were able admit when they made mistakes and took responsibility for things that didn't go well, or those things that did go well.

I define leadership as doing good things through people; having humility makes you human and approachable. This creates an environment or culture of sharing and a willingness to admit mistakes. There are many other components that we'll talk about regarding humility, but admitting mistakes is one of the most critical. Speak the truth and admit when you're wrong!

Wright

How do you define humility?

Amundson

Webster's Dictionary is very good at saying what humility is *not:* "It is not proud, haughty, arrogant, or assertive." And while that's helpful on one hand, I like to look at what humility *is*. And I have formed an acronym that has six components to it that forms the word HUMBLE.

The first letter is H for Honesty, which includes a willingness to admit your mistakes and to tell the truth. The second letter is U for Universe, and that implies your ability to see that there's something greater than yourself. The M stands for Modesty, which means a willingness to support others or lift them up. The B stands for Belief in yourself—you must have strong convictions to move an organization forward into the future toward a vision. The L is for Listening, which is always important. Seek out opinions and listen before your opinion is given. Finally the E is for Empathy, and that goes toward understanding and anticipating how other people will feel.

Admitting mistakes, believing that others often have answers better than your own, seeking out others' opinions, and listening with empathy are some of the key characteristics of being an effective, humble leader today.

Wright

How did you get interested in this concept?

Amundson

Probably at a very young age! My curiosity in leadership began when I observed friends of mine, growing up in a small town, who were able to influence people. There were people who wanted to follow them. While I had some success in that area, I wasn't always successful. So, I wondered what the underlying ingredients to being a leader were and how does one become a leader? I thought that you always had to look as though you knew the answers, even if you didn't. Admitting mistakes or not knowing something was a sign of weakness in my mind. But, as I took on leadership roles, I realized this could not be further from the truth. In fact, the opposite was true. People do not want perfection, they want humanness—they want to relate better to people who are like us. We connect with people who do not try to be perfect; their imperfections are endearing and we want to help them succeed *because* of their willingness to be like us.

So I want to reach out to those leaders whose egos and insecurities get in the way of relating well to others, to convince them to let go of the need to look perfect. A big way to start this journey is by understanding and following—those six HUMBLE characteristics: Honesty, looking to the Universe, showing Modesty, Believing in yourself, Listening, and Empathizing.

Wright

How do you know if you are a humble leader?

Amundson

There are at least two ways to assess your level of humility. The first way is by completing a "humility assessment," a tool I developed that makes seven statements about humility allowing the participant to answer on a Likert scale with one representing "never showing that characteristic" and five representing "always showing that characteristic."

The first statement on this scale is your willingness to admit mistakes and tell the truth. The next is your willingness to use other people's ideas over your own. The third is your willingness to listen fully before giving your own thoughts. The fourth is your ability to anticipate how others might feel about decisions made that affect them. The fifth is a belief in a power greater than yourself. The sixth is an ability to praise and give credit to others for work well done. And finally, your ability to get your own needs met.

This last statement sounds strange in a humility assessment, but you need to understand what you want and try to get your needs met because humility does not imply weakness, it does not imply becoming a doormat for others to walk all over; but rather, understanding your needs and getting those met.

The second way to assess your level of humility as a leader is by observing the people who report to you. Are they willing to admit mistakes? Do they take responsibility for their mistakes without blaming others? Are they good listeners? Are they open to change? The people who report to you are often a reflection upon your own style. You'll know if you're a humble leader by the way they act. Also remember to check in with yourself periodically and ask these questions: Are my first thoughts always about myself? Are they about others? How thoughtful am I? I do believe that you can learn to get better at this.

Wright

What can you do to become more humble?

Amundson

I think sometimes it's an ego-check—you need to check in with yourself and ask, "Is this about me? Or is this about others?" The big one I keep using over and over is this willingness to admit your mistakes, to tell the truth in front of others, and to listen—to become a better listener. Boy, this is such a tough component for most people because we're not comfortable with silence; we like to fill in moments of silence and so we sometimes talk over people. If you can force yourself to hear them first before you give your opinion, that's definitely a strength. The fact that you care about what people are saying, you tell the truth even when the consequences may be high, and you see yourself as a servant to others all indicate you have great leadership characteristics. You understand that it isn't about you but how you can lift others up. So check in with your ego now and then by asking these reflective questions.

Wright

Is one born humble? Can you start as a child—can it be learned?

Amundson

With the right mindset this can definitely be learned. As children our thoughts and behaviors are more self-centered, which represents the opposite of humility. There is a common saying among three-year-olds, "What's mine is mine, and what's yours is mine!" Teenagers are also classic examples of being egocentric—they're dancing between dependence on their parents and independence from them. Many of their behaviors are self-centered. They glance at themselves in the mirror whenever they can and spend hours deciding what outfit to wear to school. Their focus is on themselves more than the world around them. While these actions are natural, parents play a critical role in helping them look beyond themselves and be secure in admitting their mistakes. If the parent is role modeling humble behavior in a family setting, the child will pick up on this mindset and begin to think and act this way as well.

My journey toward becoming more humble was jump-started as I became a mother and I realized that my life now was truly second to these two wonderful, beautiful daughters who entered my life. Becoming a parent is a definite reality check.

Wright

Can you be too humble as a leader?

Amundson

Yes, if you recall in the movie *Back to the Future*, Michael J. Fox's father, George McFly, is a gentleman who admits his mistakes and who helps other people. He has all of the characteristics in my assessment except the very last, which is the ability to get his own needs met, and because of that, he's an ineffective leader. He doesn't have beliefs, convictions, and goals that are strong because he tends to blow with the wind or say things that will keep him out of trouble. You cannot be an effective leader when you don't understand where you're headed and you don't stay strong in a conviction of where you want to go. George McFly is more concerned about what others think of him and the "correct" thing to say versus the "right" thing to say.

Wright

Who are some of the humble leaders of today?

Amundson

What's really interesting is that you don't hear about them! There could definitely be some celebrities—I do believe that Oprah Winfrey has humility because I've seen her willingness to admit mistakes and not try to be "perfect" on her television show. And I know there are many other celebrities who have those qualities, but it's more difficult to see them in the spotlight.

Probably the best question to ask that will uncover these leaders is, "Where are some incredibly good things being done and no leader stepping forward to take credit for them?" That's where humble leadership is taking place. And that could be anywhere. It could be a teacher or the mayor of your town, a chief financial officer of an organization, a nurse, a politician, a salesperson—it doesn't matter what field they're in, it's people who are doing good things through people and they're not stepping forward to take the credit.

Wright

I remember a very popular song several years ago: "It's Hard to Stay Humble when You're Perfect in Every Way." So how does a leader stay humble?

Amundson

One way is to continue to read, read, read. As a matter of fact, Robert Greenleaf is a well-known leader in this field of servant leadership. There's material that he has written that continually prompts readers to ask questions and evaluate themselves. I think questions are so important in learning, developing, and changing.

The first question I've asked myself is, "What is keeping me from being humble and admitting my mistakes and telling the truth to my employees?" So, "What is it?"

The second question I might ask is, "What am I afraid of? What is the worst thing that could happen if I begin to take on these characteristics?"

The next question is, "What would be the best thing that could happen if I took on these characteristics of humility?"

Then, "What would I need to do to feel safe trying these new things?"

And, "How can I be more open to others' ideas? How can I detach from being tied to an idea and accept better ideas?"

"How can I become a better listener? How can I praise others and see the good in others' ideas? How can I become a servant to my staff?"

And I firmly believe in the concept of a power greater than ourselves, so when these questions are put out there, the amazing thing that happens is the answers appear. This is reflected in the concept of when the student is ready the teacher will appear. But your heart and soul really have to feel the need for these answers before the answers will appear. Answers will come in the form of a mentor, in the form of an article or a book. Just asking the questions with humility is when the magic happens. You observe and want to change, and that's a wonderful place to be.

Wright

How does a humble leader make a company more profitable? Are there examples where humility improved the bottom line?

Amundson

One of the best examples of how humility impacts the profitability of a company is found in a book called *Good to Great* by Jim Collins. Jim spent five years researching the question, what makes companies that are good, become great, and sustain that greatness? Jim's team combed through piles of data looking for companies that had a "specific pattern of fifteen years of cumulative stock returns at or below the general stock market, followed by a transition point that then led to a cumulative return at least three times the market over the next fifteen years". Through his research, he discovered that these great companies all had leaders at the transition point who shared two primary characteristics: a mix of humility and will. These leaders are called Level Five Leaders because they show a drive to help the company succeed ahead of their individual need to succeed, and a great deal of humility in that process! Jim explains, "The Level Five Leaders were self-effacing, quiet, reserved, even shy. These leaders are a paradoxical blend of personal humility and professional will. They are more like Lincoln and Socrates than Patton or Caesar."

The bottom line result was that these companies were able to return six times the dollar investment than other companies, *and* they sustained it for over fifteen years. I can't think of anything much harder than this to prove that humility actually hits the bottom line.

Wright

Why do you think that humility is more important than the numerous other traits of an effective leader?

Amundson

I don't know that one is more important than the other—I think it's a condition of priority. I know leaders need to have a vision, communicate that vision effectively, and take risks. But the foundation of humility is what allows you to be open to ideas and to learn to become better at communicating, creating a vision, and taking risks. Humility is what opens up doors for better learning.

I like to use the metaphor of a house. If you're building a house the foundation is probably the most critical component. If the foundation is faulty or defective, the house will lean and eventually not sustain itself. This is how it is with humility. When you have a foundation of integrity, honesty, and humility, you have a strong house, and a strong base or character as a human being. I've seen so many people rise in organizations who don't have humility, yet they can communicate, articulate a vision, and take risks; but eventually they all get found out. They collapse, just as a house collapses because they did not have a strong foundation.

So it's not that those other characteristics aren't important, they are important; but the foundation and basis on which to grow is humility and honesty.

Wright

How will my organization or I be hurt if I do not choose a humble attitude?

Amundson

As I mentioned, if you, as the leader, do not have this as a foundation, and you are communicating with people, you're going to find that you create a culture where people don't admit their mistakes, and they are unwilling to listen to others. They will not praise others and lift others up. As a leader, you create the culture that reports to you, and if those things are not in place, you cannot be as competitive, especially in a global economy where every nuance matters in a business. The leader sets the culture or the way that people interact with each other. If the leader has an arrogant attitude, it will lead to distrust, withholding information, and blaming, all of which can lead to the demise of a company, especially in a highly competitive global marketplace.

Wright

I had an incident a few days ago where one of the employees of the company that I own called to tell me good news about another employee who had made a lot of sales, her first few sales. I thought, great, this is going to be such a great conversation. She spent about three minutes telling me about the other person's sales, and then she spent the next forty-five minutes telling me how much she had helped her do it!

Amundson

Okay, it became obvious what the point of that conversation was.

Wright

I get it—a manifestation of a low self-image and someone who was *not* humble.

Amundson

Exactly. And if this person were leading others, her behavior would negatively affect her team because she is obviously thinking of others and praising others, but has her self-interests ahead of anything else. She is insecure in her abilities and must continually prove herself competent to others. If she only understood that her success is directly tied to the success of her team—it is not about her.

Wright

So how I can assess my level of humility?

Amundson

It goes back to the humility assessment that I mentioned earlier in this chapter, and it's ranked on a score of thirty-five points possible. Once you have a better understanding and a base line of where you are, we can work through each of these seven characteristics and help you get better. So to me, the best way is to look at these seven characteristics and ask yourself honestly how you rank and where the trouble spots are for you. Where are the areas in which you do well already? We always want to encourage you to continue to do the good things over and over, and then to look at those areas of weakness and ask for help—and again, it's a sign of humility to ask for help, and it all begins with that!

Wright

Very interesting. I have published several books on leadership and characteristics of leadership, and I've had conversations about *servant* leadership, but you're the only person I've talked with who has specifically defined humility as well as you have defined it here today.

I really do appreciate all this time you've spent with me answering these questions.

Amundson

Thank you, David, it's been a pleasure. I believe very strongly that humility is a characteristic that we miss in studying leadership. Being an effective communicator, having a vision, and taking risk are all critical as well, but there must be a foundation of humility in a leader that will enhance that leader's ability to communicate, create a vision, and take risks. Humility is the foundation to successful leadership. Without it, any other characteristic is just frosting, if you will, with no cake underneath!

About Diane Amundson

DIANE AMUNDSON has a passion for working with people who want to develop as leaders and organizations that want to develop their people. She is a graduate of the Carlson School of Management and served as Adjunct Professor of Organizational Development at Winona State University. She has worked with thousands of individuals and organizations since 1992 in the areas of communication, team building, and leadership development. Download her humility assessment free at www.dianeamundson.com.

Diane Amundson
Diane Amundson & Associates
24456 County Road 9
Winona MN 55987
507.452.2232
diane@dianeamundson.com
www.dianeamundson.com

Chapter Ten

An interview with...

Dr. Jo Anne Bishop

Living Your Potential Through Integrated Focus

David Wright (Wright)

Today we're talking with Jo Anne Bishop, PhD, founder and CEO of Crossing Bridges & Associates, a coaching, consulting, and conflict mediation company located in Honolulu, Hawaii. A motivational and inspirational speaker, Certified Professional Coach, licensed psychotherapist, and certified hypnotherapist, Jo Anne reaches a national and international client base in the entertainment, customer service, real estate related industries and banking. Her coaching clients include CEOs, entrepreneurs, senior executives, and top producers. She specializes in one-on-one coaching, conflict mediation in family owned businesses, and the corporate setting. Jo Anne has also been a consultant and trainer to state, local, and federal governments.

Her mission is to empower each client with the ability to access the powerhouse of unlimited potential that lies within the conscious and subconscious mind. She believes that this potential is realized through harnessing the elements of passion, intuition, and creativity aligned with clear strategic decision-making, intention to succeed, and personal accountability.

She holds graduate degrees in Counseling, Psychology, and Public Policy and Administration. Her organizational memberships include the International Coach Federation, International Association of Coaches, American Society of Training and Development, American Association of Psychotherapy and Medical Hypnosis, International Speakers Bureau, and the Hawaii Speakers Network.

Dr. Bishop, welcome to *Success Strategies!*

Jo Anne C. Bishop (Bishop)

Thank you, David; I am very delighted to be here.

Wright

You are a Certified Professional Coach. How can coaching be a tool for success?

Bishop

Coaching can provide a dynamic addition to success strategies by empowering clients with a comprehensive framework that utilizes tools, which accelerate learning development and competencies in a comprehensive, measurable objective environment. The coaching process provides enhanced feedback, support, confidence, and empowerment to the client. Each client's program is uniquely tailored to address individual needs, goals, and vision. It can be utilized individually or within a corporate environment to integrate the individual's goals within the corporate vision.

This base provides a platform that enables the client to address and explore latent talents, ideas, and creativity while focusing on current goals, decision-making, and skill development. Through this unbiased approach, a structure is developed to propel the client beyond his or her current state of development. The focal point of this formulated plan is to capitalize on the client's talents and strengths. This plan defines subsequent steps to success, delivering a concrete measurable approach that provides clarity and innovative problem solving.

Within the context of my coaching, I provide the tools that are necessary to access inherent creativity, intuition, and the subconscious mind. All of these elements aid the conscious mind on the road to competency and success, which allows the individual the opportunity to explore his or her capacity for change and development. The intention of all coaching methods is to support the client by increasing self-awareness and self-confidence through a concrete validation of the client's talents and accomplishments.

Coaching has been found to increase productivity, job satisfaction, and overall life experience. Harvard Business School cited a 2004 study by Right Management Consultants. The study found that 86 percent of the companies surveyed used coaching as a way to develop leadership skills in their managers. They also found that there was a 570 percent return on this corporate investment through increased production and employee retention. In the same study, IBM reported employing sixty certified coaches on staff to enhance employee performance.

I'm passionate about the contribution coaching can make in a person's life and the impact that it can have on organizations as a secondary benefit.

Wright

Specifically, how does coaching benefit successful high achievers?

Bishop

I think it is important to delineate the qualities of a high achiever. The high achiever is very different from the average achiever. High achievers are curious, self-directed, self-reflective, willing to take risks, and manage their time effectively with an innate ability to efficiently prioritize tasks. They are totally committed to their goals and love the learning process. The outcome is a byproduct of their passion to learn and succeed.

A study completed by Global Matrix, an international survey company that looks at individual performance, found that approximately 80 percent of the work force in most companies were either average achievers or below average, leaving the remaining 20 percent as high achievers. The percentage spread puts the high achiever in an isolated working environment. Management values them as leaders and producers. The high achiever's isolation is increased by the company's reluctance to disturb the status quo of a system, which is already successful. These two factors can leave high achievers without valuable feedback that promotes their learning development. In addition, high achievers in executive positions have far less feedback than those at the lower levels of management. This philosophy is based upon the adage "if it's not broken, don't fix it." This maintains the corporate balance, but places limitations on the high achiever's incredible potential talents, creativity, and leadership skills. Until recently, the philosophy trickled down to all levels of management and limited the development of in- house talent.

Coaching can be a dynamic change agent for the organization. Although it is usually done on a one-to-one basis, its outcome is beneficial to the entire organization. Coaching can also benefit the average achiever or underachiever by increasing employee confidence in abilities and skill levels. Coaching clarifies areas that require improvement, and provides the opportunity to remove obstacles to advancement and achievement. It stimulates the desire for improvement and offers individual motivation to reach higher levels of performance.

In September 2007, the American Society for Training and Development reported that many companies are now viewing their employees as a fundamental component of economic development. This changing attitude makes the high achiever a valuable resource for the company's expansion. Learning development programs become a vehicle for improved profit margin and return on investment. This is a vital component for the company to stay competitive in today's marketplace. Coaching provides the opportunity to explore personal development in an environment based on trust offering constructive feedback not usually available to the high achiever in the corporate setting.

Wright

What are the benefits of coaching as compared to classroom or on-the-job training?

Bishop

Coaching programs are specifically designed to meet the needs of the individual client. These programs are experiential learning processes tailored to the goals and visions of the individual, not generic company mandated training. The knowledge that is acquired through coaching is the result of the individual's self-motivation and choice. Most training programs are designed for the average employee, which places limitations on the higher achiever. In addition, classroom training has limited opportunities to measure results.

Coaching is directed by choice and accountability to the achievement of goals rather than by obligation to attend more generic training formats. All learning stimulates and activates brain cells; therefore any style of corporate learning is valuable. However, choice has been proven to be a substantial factor in the acquisition of knowledge retention, and the theoretical application of the principles gained through the learning process.

Both coaching and on the job training is usually completed on a one-to-one basis. This one-on-one learning style has proven to be more effective than group training. In a recent article, the *New York Times* reported that 80 percent of learning is informally gained by gatherings of employees "at the water cooler." Although this informal process lacks the significant components of goal setting, timelines, and accountability gained from coaching, it provides valuable feedback and an opportunity for creative problem solving on current projects. This works as a collective employee learning style but usually does not reach out to the high achiever.

I cannot over emphasize that all learning systems expand the brain's ability to work more effectively. All methods of learning are important. Coaching is a more intensified learning style that provides real time measurable results for the individual but can also be applied to a group.

Wright

What is unique about your perspective on coaching?

Bishop

My background includes expertise in business, education, psychology, and training development. I utilize all of these disciplines during coaching. The integration of these disciplines promotes the development of boundless human potential and resiliency.

Society faces many issues that seem insurmountable. Through focused attention, the solutions to these challenges can come not only from our analytical and cognitive prowess, but also from our continued desire to reach into the reservoir of creative, intuitive, and emotional intelligence.

High achievers innately use all of these aspects of intelligence. They have the ability to rebound with energy and enthusiasm in the face of challenges. This is what I just referred to as resiliency. I believe this is a skill that can be learned by others.

I am passionate about these possibilities within my fellow man and believe, with the appropriate learning processes, we can expand the unlimited potential for problem solving within all of us. My clients are trained to manifest their gifts. Incremental learning can provide steps that assist movement toward goals and visions without being overwhelmed by the process. Using the subconscious mind, the client can learn to access a flow within him or her. This supports clients' goals by reducing resistance to change.

We are living in a time of intensive brain research. This exciting new information allows us to understand the organic mechanical aspects of brain function. At the same time, science is telling us that our brains have unlimited capability to grow our talents. I encourage clients to go beyond their self-imposed limitations.

Understanding how their brain functions allow them to gain knowledge of the conscious and subconscious mind. As they begin to understand how they learn and how the brain functions intelligently, emotionally, and creatively, they can begin to utilize tools that access the powerhouse within. This knowledge creates the capability of manifesting their dreams and visions into physical reality. As I said earlier, all learning promotes a change in brain chemistry and brain cells. We can create new neural pathways through exercises that provide conscious access to both the right and left hemispheres' power and potential. I believe this approach is what makes my coaching unique.

Wright

In your presentations you speak about using creativity and intuition to unleash the powerhouse within your clients. What does this mean?

Bishop

The process of opening the door to the unlimited potential that resides in each of us is emotionally based, but we must consciously choose to open that door. Visualization and the intention to succeed, which is based in personal choice, are key components that unlock the door to that powerhouse.

Visualization is the language of the subconscious. Michelangelo said, "If I can visualize it, I can create it." Most of the great contributions to humanity have come from individuals who innately understood the process of integrating the gifts from the brain's right and left hemispheres. They allowed the intuitive inspirations of the subconscious mind to integrate with the rational analytical conscious brain and produce giant steps forward in our evolutionary process. We see them as masters. I believe we all have access to inspiration and the gifts within us. My coaching creates a systematic program that builds confidence and highlights the power within the subconscious through the intuitive and creative mind.

Intuition is the gateway to inspiration. I teach the methodology to validate intuitive inspirations incorporating them as a skill.

Wright

I thought only certain people had the power of intuition.

Bishop

It is a myth that only some individuals are intuitive and creative when in reality we all have the potential to develop this as a skill.

The right side of our brain is the part that experiences feelings such as sorrow, hurt, joy, or anger. This part of our brain has the ability to creatively imagine outcomes. Imagination can be used to visualize the completion of tasks or goals. Our dreams, both day and night, are part of this ability to access the creative capabilities of the brain.

The right brain is also the place where "gut reactions" reside. We all have gut reactions at one time or another. Most of us dismiss these feelings. A gut reaction comes from instinct. Instinct comes from a part of the brain scientists have labeled the "old brain." Instinct tells us that we are in danger. Instinct has helped mankind evolve over billions of years. The need to survive is hardwired in all of us and is a gift from generation to generation. As we evolved, our brained developed the ability to reason through this process; we genetically inherit our unique propensity for creative and scientific reasoning. This is a left-brain function.

The brain has biochemical reactions that help us to reason, feel, and perceive our reality. As mankind's brain has evolved, we have retained the instinct for survival. Intuition uses the same neuropathways as instinct, but evolved as mankind's brain took on higher levels of processing. Intuition is a process used by both hemispheres of the brain. It allows us to have impressions or inspirations that do not come from the rational mind. However, this insight from the right hemisphere gains definition through the ability of the left hemisphere to put words to the insight. As we use our intuitive talents, we begin to develop a language that becomes a conscious part of daily life. Our rational brain helps us make sense of the insight. Through understanding the dynamics of intuitive messages, we begin to validate intuition as a valuable tool and skill. There is a learning curve to all skills. The more you test your intuition and learn its signals, the more you receive. Our brains are similar to computers and both hemispheres are constantly processing and producing data. As we become aware of this process, we begin to understand the true power of the brain. The more we become aware of the subconscious and conscious interaction, the more we understand our abilities to strategically problem-solve.

There is a misunderstanding that we use only 10 percent of our brain's capacity. Our brains actually function as a single organ and use 100 percent to function. However, we only understand a small percentage of the brain's ability. Each part of the brain is activated by different internal and external stimuli that affect both hemispheres. Science is now conducting the research that is providing us with a glimpse of the brain's capability. We have over three billion brain cells. New research indicates that these brain cells can activate and expand our ability to continually learn new skills without age limit.

Benjamin Franklin, George Patton, Bill Gates, and Albert Einstein believed that their rational minds were the receptacles for the great inspiration of the intuitive creative mind. Their problem-solving abilities were exponentially increased by their receptiveness to subconscious impressions and inspirations. This ability can be learned.

My seminars teach people how to reach beyond the limits of the rational mind. Through experiential exercises, participants learn to develop their intuitive perception. The enthusiasm created during the seminar as participants see immediate improvement in their ability to perceive information, previously unknown to their rational minds, is apparent. When verified through immediate feedback the participants begin to understand that intuitive ability is a skill that can be learned.

Wright

You also speak about the importance of using fear as a creative force. Isn't fear a negative emotion and an obstacle to success? How do you use fear as a creative force?

Bishop

Using fear creatively can be a success strategy. Fear is common to everyone and if severe, activates an instinct within us called a flight or fight response. This response saturates our bodies with powerful hormones. These hormones push us toward survival.

We can harness fear and these chemicals in a positive manner. Most people do not understand what to do when they become frightened. Fear has different stages. At the least, fear can be as simple as anxiety about speaking to a group and as severe as fear for one's life. Fear is usually associated with negative thinking and can be immobilizing. Fear moves to feelings of immobilization as people deny that they are afraid. We are taught to ignore our fears in early childhood by parents who were taught the same thing by their parents. Children are not taught that they have options when confronted by fear. This creates a sense of helplessness that lingers into adulthood. Increasing the number of options available to deal with fear reduces the feeling of helplessness as choices are made to move forward and take risks. When asked by corporate consultants what stops employees from moving to the next level of advancement, the number one response is fear of failure.

Fear can be harnessed as a powerful force and transformed into creativity. We need the skill to learn how to embrace fear and develop courage to face our fears. Courage transforms fear to a higher level of functioning. Fear can be owned and used as a propellant for action. A framework can be developed to harness fear through systematic behaviors and skills that deal with the fear. We can learn to identify fear and take action to transform it into creativity and action. This process transforms fear into the powerful ally of creativity.

Wright

In layman's terms, what are the two hemispheres of the brain and what are their functions?

Bishop

I talked earlier in our interview about the right and left brain hemispheres. As I stated, the right brain is the center of feelings, imagination, and non-sequential reasoning.

The right hemisphere sees things holistically and randomly. It is the seat of emotion, imagination, and inspiration. It is the conduit for creativity, intuition, instinct, and the subconscious.

The left hemisphere is the seat of analytical, logical, rational decision-making where language, mathematics, and deductive reasoning reside. The more we develop the ability to consciously access both of the brain's hemispheres, the more neural connections and pathways are activated. As we further our capacity through learning, greater skills are developed. Reduction of fear and stress that relates to the right hemisphere increases ability to create a sense of peace, empowerment, and balance, increasing the power of the left hemisphere to bring clarity and wisdom to goal- and decision-making.

Science is now defining the differences between the conscious and subconscious mind. These definitions are relevant to the fields of coaching, human development, and training. We now know that the rational cognitive mind cannot be separated from the emotional mind. Learning involves both hemispheres and the conscious and subconscious mind. Challenging both hemispheres through the activation of underdeveloped brain cells can provide clients the required edge to be successful with mind, body, and spirit in the marketplace.

Wright

You talk about harnessing the power of the brain through the integration of the conscious and the subconscious. What does this mean and how is it important in your coaching strategy?

Bishop

Knowledge and understanding empower us on a multidimensional level. We talked earlier about how learning changes brain chemistry. If we know and understand the unique functioning of our brains, we can begin to feel confident in our ability to change. This confidence increases our ability to take risks and embrace challenge. The high achiever does this automatically without resistance.

The conscious part of us is aware of our reality. We use the conscious to set goals, analyze problems, and set timelines. The subconscious dreams about what we can be and provides inspiration that can become flashes of clarity. This is sometimes called a peak experience. A peak experience or "being in the flow" is really a merging of the conscious and subconscious. Most people describe this as an elevated knowing or understanding. It creates a feeling of oneness with others and ourselves. These peak experiences are an attainable state of being that the average person can learn to reproduce. This state of mind increases performance levels and productivity with a sense of ease.

Through new technology we are becoming aware that the brain has plasticity. Plasticity is the brain's ability to expand and grow in skill level by utilizing unused brain cells as a resource. Through the practice of various learning techniques we can increase the capacity to activate unused brainpower. These new scientific findings are important to me because they provide the opportunity to relate scientific evidence to my clients that validates the notion that they are limited only by their own thinking and decision-making. The intention to learn how to interconnect and access the power within the two hemispheres creates an opportunity for clients to gain previously unimagined levels of achievement. Intention is an interconnected desire that unites both hemispheres to claim a goal and move toward it without resistance—this is the perfect combination of the two hemispheres working together with the individual's conscious intention.

Wright

How do you coach individuals to meet challenges?

Bishop

The word "challenge" creates feelings of dread or fear in some individuals. It can produce a feeling of being overwhelmed. This feeling is precipitated by feelings of inadequacy and helplessness. I have worked with many people who believe that they do not have the skills to meet most challenges.

I coach my clients to break down challenges into incremental parts. This allows challenges to become manageable. When challenges become manageable, confidence is restored. This is the first step in the development of resiliency. Resiliency can be learned and expanded. Challenges can be solved through commitment, accountability, creativity, and the development of action plans. Resiliency is learned through trusting yourself.

The ability to visualize the successful outcome to a challenge is essential. We need to stimulate the courage to move toward challenges with a plan, see the successful outcome, and learn from each situation.

All of the things that I have just addressed are components of resiliency. The ideas of failure and perfection need to be removed from our vocabulary. They do not appear as limitations to the successful person. Embracing positive outcomes with the intention to succeed is definitely a success strategy.

Wright

What are the common traits that high achievers possess?

Bishop

High achievers are extremely resilient and curious. They are able to embrace challenges, looking within themselves for new ways of thinking and problem solving. They are usually accountable for their mistakes without making excuses. They take responsibility for their errors and take ownership of their skill gaps, which allows them to experience learning as an enjoyable process. Most high achievers are solution-oriented self-starters with an intention to succeed. They approach challenges with confidence and enthusiasm. I believe they access the subconscious mind more easily than the average person, thereby producing inspired ideas and inventions. They are demanding of themselves, and have a tendency to believe that what they achieve is not extraordinary. When it comes to success, their inability to validate accomplishments leaves them lacking in self-reflection and self-knowledge.

In many ways, their standards are so high that they believe what they achieve is the norm. Although they have a great desire for feedback, they rarely received it. Feedback is limited because their peers tend to elevate them and subsequently hesitate to provide constructive criticism.

My approach differs with high achievers in many ways. As a coach, you must understand and have empathy for the commitment it takes to accomplish the goals set by a high achiever. High achievers must also be taught the art of validation because if they lack this skill, they become demanding of others and themselves. The key to working with high achievers is providing constructive relevant feedback while stimulating curiosity through challenging them on all levels.

Wright

This has been a great conversation and I have really learned a lot today. I'm certain that our readers will. It's very interesting the way that your coaching really is unique!

Bishop

Thank you, David; it's been a pleasure speaking with you.

About Jo Anne Bishop

DR. JO ANNE BISHOP is founder and CEO of Crossing Bridges & Associates. She is a Certified Professional Coach with a national and international client base. A top performer and leader in her field, she brings twenty years of expertise to coaching, communications, organizational psychology, and training development. She completed a highly successful psychotherapy and consulting practice in Beverly Hills and Long Beach, California, to create Crossing Bridges and Associates. A gifted speaker, presenter, and coach, she has developed dynamic experientially based programs that propel clients to the leading edge in the competitive market place. Her programs integrate goal-setting, strategic decision-making, and accountability with the power of the intuitive/creative mind. Her credentials include graduate degrees in Counseling Psychology, Public Policy, and Administration. She holds certifications in education and clinical hypnotherapy. Dr. Bishop's professional memberships include: The American Association of Family Therapists, the American Association of Psychotherapy and Medical Hypnosis, the International Coach Federation, International Coach Association, American Society of Training and Development, the International Speakers Bureau, and the Hawaii Speakers Network. She and her husband reside in the beautiful Hawaiian Islands.

Jo Anne C. Bishop, PhD, MPA
Crossing Bridges & Associates
6800 Kalanianaole Highway, #126
Honolulu, HI 96825
808.772.0266 (office)
562.760.3009 (cell)
crossingbridges@hawaii.rr.com
www.execandbusinesscoaching.com

Chapter Eleven

An interview with...

Alice Collier

Television's Fascinating Lady

David Wright (Wright)

Alice Collier is a celebrated television news journalist who has gone one-on-one with three U.S. Presidents and countless celebrities. She is a warm and charismatic personal Life Coach who has positively influenced the lives of hundreds of women. She is the face and inspiration behind a growing, faith-based, non-profit organization that helps single mothers and their children in crisis.

Alice Collier's life has been full and impressive—a life that still has many chapters remaining to unfold. Through it all she has found success at every stop and every endeavor she's pursued. Now she is ready to share with us her recipe for success.

Welcome to *Success Strategies,* Alice.

Alice, you've had an extremely fascinating career in so many different and unrelated areas and have been very successful in each and every one. How is that?

Alice Collier (Collier)

Passion—I've been so passionate about the endeavors I've chosen to pursue. I've been very selective of the jobs and the causes I've become associated with. I don't jump into everything that comes my way. I am really an intuitive person. I have to feel it—I have to feel right about what I'm doing and feel that I'm doing my very best while serving the greatest good of others.

Let me give you an example: my television career. It is truly a miracle that I was ever on television. I've never taken a journalism course in my life. I was studying to be a lawyer. During my junior year of college I suffered a disastrous event. My father tragically died in a freak accident in our home. Later that year, my mother was asked to be a guest on a Detroit television show to talk about running his company. I went with her to the television station.

I walked into the newsroom during a breaking news story. A tanker truck had just exploded on a major highway in downtown Detroit. I could feel the high energy in that space. It was incredibly exciting to me. I felt like I belonged. There were news crews running all over the place trying to prepare for live shots from the scene. The producers, anchors, reporters, and photographers were screaming and yelling, throwing papers, and just going wild. I said to myself, "This is what I want to do! I'm going to do this!"

My mother was not thrilled with my decision. She said, "No, you are going to law school. Either you go to law school or else you're on your own."

I then said, "See ya!" I was passionate about it. I threw caution to the wind and began to pursue a career in broadcast journalism. I landed my first on-air television job about nine months later. I loved it! I worked really hard too. I went from making minimum wage in a small market to earning a six-figure salary in a major market within three years. That's rare; it's truly a miracle. I wanted to do it, I believed I could do it, and I was willing to work hard to see my dream become a reality.

Wright

Of all the interesting things you've done in your professional career, what ranks as your biggest and most significant accomplishment?

Collier

Being "a voice" for people who have no voice. I've spoken out for innocent victims of senseless crimes when nobody else would listen to their cries for help. I've called for justice when the KKK or other hate groups tried to threaten and intimidate large sectors of my community. I've demanded accountability when elected officials wrangled over mere pennies to pay schoolteachers while children were denied an education because of a massive union strike.

Yet out of all the lives I've touched, I believe my most significant moment was a very personal television story I covered in 1986. I'm not even sure how many people even watched it. I do know that one person watched it and it changed his world.

I went to cover an ordinary story about the opening of a new children's wing at a local hospital. Keep in mind, back then technology was not as advanced as it is today; we didn't have laptop computers or the Internet or even cell phones with cameras. I was getting ready to go live on television when a nurse asked me if I could have my cameraman pan over the audience and get a view of a particular little patient. This two-year old girl remarkably survived a near fatal car crash on an extremely icy West Michigan road. After being pulled from the wreckage by the jaws-of-life emergency rescue tools, her dad was rushed to a different hospital. He lay clinging to life miles and miles away from his beloved daughter. The little girl was too young and too traumatized to have a phone conversation with her father, so he thought the worst. Despite assurances from his wife and family, he did not believe that his daughter was alive. He thought people were deceiving him in an effort to keep his spirits up. He started losing his will to live.

I personally decided to change the whole focus of my live shot and put all the attention on their story. Near the end of my segment I looked into the camera, talking directly to this dad (I was told he was watching) and said, "Ed, here is your daughter. She is very much alive and she needs you to hurry up and get well so the two of you can play together again soon."

The father's nurses said he was so touched that he began to cry. (Just telling this story still makes me well up with tears.) The station's phones lit up with calls from viewers. We received so many inquiries that the family's plight to survive became one of our leading stories the next day. Local radio stations and newspapers picked it up as well. The critically injured father wanted to meet me so I went to the hospital the next day. Fighting back tears, he thanked me for giving him hope and the motivation to fight through the pain of an extensive recovery. His doctor said that if it weren't for me being "a voice" for this family that Ed may not have lived another day.

Wright

What was it like interviewing three U.S. Presidents? It had to be somewhat intimidating, right?

Collier

Petrifying is more like it! I interviewed President Gerald Ford, President Jimmy Carter, and President Ronald Reagan. (I'm really giving away my age, aren't I? That's okay.) I must tell you, being in the presence of a United States president is electrifying. No matter who he is or which political party he represented as President, each one was one of the most powerful men in the world. That in and of itself is incredible. I was in awe of their position and the respect each of these presidents received.

There's a night and day difference between seeing a president on television and being in the same room with him. A television set is unable to capture the vibrant atmosphere in the place. There's the buzz of the Secret Service, the dedication of the President's staff, and the public displays of patriotism from the crowds of people that gather everywhere he goes, making it an exciting experience.

My knees were knocking and my heart was pounding during a press conference with then Vice President George H. W. Bush. He was a tough interview that day. The presence of the national press corps made it even more nerve-racking. I was only a local reporter (one, I may add, with guts). I asked him a question he refused to answer, but I would not sit down until he responded. Needless to say, he was not very happy with me. The Secret Service started inching toward me; I just stood there and respectfully reiterated the question. It was in reference to a massive labor union strike throughout the Midwest. He and President Reagan kept making the statement that Americans were "better off now than we were four years ago" and I wanted to know how they could make such a campaign remark when tens of thousands of blue-collar workers were suffering major pay cuts. He finally commented, and I sat back down. Well-known ABC News Anchor Carol Simpson leaned over to me and said, "Good going girl!"

Wright

You made your mark as an acclaimed television news journalist who easily could have gone on to a bigger stage, yet decided to go in a different direction. What prompted the change?

Collier

Life happened! I really wanted to have a family. I went from investigating hardened criminals and dishonest politicians to birthing babies. What a hoot! My New York agent was fit to be tied. I turned down an offer to anchor in Los Angeles in order to work in Orlando for much less money and start a family. It was not a lucrative deal for her, but it was the best choice for me. I learned long ago to live my dreams instead of someone else's.

My life has not turned out the way I once anticipated. Remember, I was expected and preparing to become a lawyer and stay close to home. Plan A didn't work for me so I designed Plan B. I often tell women that their Plan B is often the best plan. Look at me! I'm raising three amazing sons in a sunny, warm part of the country. I was able to juggle both work and kids for a season, even hosting my own television show for six years. I also have gone on to pursue worthwhile causes in my community, which has brought me both accomplishment and great personal satisfaction.

Wright

Times have changed for the better for women in television news. There are more female news anchors today than when you first broke into the business. What were some of the obstacles you had to overcome in what was once a male-dominated field?

Collier

The biggest hurtle I had to overcome was to be taken seriously. After I decided to be a news reporter, I looked for an internship at the Detroit television stations. One of the network affiliate stations was accepting applications; I applied. I was interviewed by the station's chief investigative reporter. I'll never forget it. I wore an off-white, fashionable wool suit, high heels, I had long red nails, and my hair was perfectly coiffed. I really wanted be an intern in the investigative unit. During the interview he looked at the way I was dressed and said to me, "Alice, you will never make it in this business."

I was insulted and replied, "Why not!"

He answered, "Because you are too pretty and too well dressed. Nobody will ever take you seriously."

"Not only will I make it in this business," I said, "but one day I'll be after your job!" Sure enough, he hired me on the spot. I went from working as a gofer in that unpaid internship to a major market news anchor in just three short years.

I paid my dues though by working twice as hard as my male co-workers. Consequently, I earned the respect of those men around me. I became accustomed to being the only female in a room crowded with male colleagues.

Once a local male politician tried to either take advantage of or make fun of that fact. He went around the room shaking every one else's hand but mine. He attempted to kiss my hand, which I believe was highly unprofessional. Well, I wasn't falling for his good looks or charisma. I squeezed down on his hand so hard that he winced. He got the message. I wanted to be valued and taken seriously as a journalist. We eventually ended up having a profound respect for each other.

"Don't be fooled by her beautiful smile and charming demeanor," he later forewarned a colleague before a live interview. He stated, "Alice is a bulldog. She asks tough questions and won't let up until you've answered them."

Wright

What challenges did you encounter making the transition from the celebrity of a news personality to the anonymity of a Life Coach? I'm sure the rewards of each are quite different.

Collier

It was a huge transition, but it was made sweeter by the birth of my sons. I never expected to leave television. I love television news. Every single day is different and every story brings a distinctive set of circumstances and perspectives. I was always out where the action was instead of being stuck behind a desk. I thrive on that kind of fast-paced, high energy broadcast news.

I had every intention of going back to work after my first child. Toward the end of my maternity leave, I took my precious infant to the station to show him off. A reporter held my baby while I went into my news director's office to say hello. He said he was excited that I was returning in a week. I started to sob. (Those weren't crocodile tears either; this was sincere emotion.)

"What's wrong?" he asked sympathetically.

I said, "I love television, but I love my son more and I just now realized that I can't come back to work." I opted to stay home and raise my children, which, by the way, is the hardest job I've ever had.

Yes, it was difficult at first. I am very driven and was such a career woman. My infant was unable to appreciate my dedication and sacrifices as my viewers had done. But the love I felt for him (and later his younger brothers) was so intense that it extinguished the desire to be a celebrity. I matured experientially as a mother and spiritually as a person.

As a result of that very private decision, I've learned to welcome transition as a positive occurrence in life. I've become skilled at creating more of what I want in my life and excluding what no longer fits me and my family. So, I've had to make some alterations in both my professional life and my personal life. The adventure has been one big reward.

Wright

You are now regarded as one of the better-known Life Coaches, and over the years you have worked almost exclusively with women of all ages and from varying education and social backgrounds. Why just women, when everyone, it seems, could benefit from a good, knowledgeable Life Coach?

Collier

One of my protégés says that uplifting women comes as naturally to me as breathing. Inspiring and encouraging women is what I believe I was destined to do in life. I understand the challenges that women face. I know firsthand what it is like to experience the pain of abuse, divorce, financial loss, loneliness, and the death of a loved one. These experiences have given me a clear perspective on the restorative power that exists within all of us.

My deepest desire is to empower women to rise above their circumstances to become better instead of bitter. I trust that by sharing my personal experiences, women will find the hope they need to transform their lives positively . . . one step at a time.

Wright

You couldn't come as far as you have in life without good role models to look up to. Who were some of those people who had the greatest influence on your life?

Collier

My father and my maternal grandmother have had the most influence on me. I miss them both very much.

My father, Kenneth Edwards, was a highly successful insurance salesman. "Shoot for the moon because even if you miss, you'll land among the stars," that's the attitude my father always conveyed. He loved me. He thought that I could do anything I wanted to do. With that combination of love and support, I started to believe I could reach my dreams even at an early age. I discovered that if I focused on my goals rather than any limitations, I would hit the mark each and every time.

As for my grandma, Adalene Pryor, she was the classiest lady I've ever met. Oh, she was gorgeous too. When I was a child, I thought she looked like Elizabeth Taylor. Men would swoon when she walked in a room. She sewed automobile upholstery at a Cadillac factory in Detroit. She was proof that class is not inherited—class is a learned behavior. Ann Landers wrote, "The most affluent blueblood can be totally without class while the descendant of a Welsh miner may ooze class from every pore." People frequently ask me how I acquired such social grace. I learned it from my grandma. She taught me how to be a respectable, confident lady. She never called me by my real name; she and my grandpa always called me, "Princess." And, I believed I was born into a noble family.

Wright

Today you serve as positive and successful role model, especially for women—a responsibility you take extreme pride in. What do you think a person's initial impressions of you are when they meet you for the first time?

Collier

When men and women first meet me they tend to just stare at me. I often giggle. They usually indicate they're staring because they think I'm beautiful and very sophisticated. A distinguished national television correspondent described me as *"unforgettable."* She mentioned that I am tall, slender, and immaculately groomed and gorgeous. And just yesterday an acquaintance described me to another woman as being beautiful and elegant with a wonderfully big heart. You know what? I am genuinely flattered and also embarrassed by people's reaction. I must admit that I am unique looking; I'm a nice blend of different ethnic groups. However, my grandma, whom I thought was gorgeous, always told me, "pretty is as pretty does." She meant that if I was vain or acted stuck up, no one would ever consider me attractive.

I grew up believing my outward appearance only enhances me rather than defines me. My character and integrity are the qualities I've always valued most. Once people get to know me, I truly hope they find they're drawn to me because I'm a good person and an outstanding mother.

Wright

Over the years you have been and continue to be involved in charitable and civic work, ranging from inner city ministries to established social organizations to your most recent endeavor, "Angels Trace." That's a tough balancing act. How do you find time to do all that?

Collier

It's a priority. I make the time. When I was in elementary school, my father once took me to a soup kitchen in one of Detroit's most underprivileged neighborhoods on Thanksgiving. The experience left an indelible mark in my soul.

My father wanted to drop off a donation to the woman who ran the soup kitchen (from her small tenement I might add). My eyes grew big and my mouth dropped open as I walked through the room. I had never seen such poverty before. My father asked me not to gawk at the homeless people who were there eating.

Walking back to the car, my father said to me, "Alice, we're no better than those people you saw inside. We're just a paycheck away from where they are."

I didn't believe that, but I realized he was trying to make a point and his point was well received. He wanted me to be grateful for all the blessings I have received and to always help those people who were less fortunate. That was many, many years ago, and to this day I'm still doing all I can to support the disadvantaged. It's who I am.

Wright

Angels Trace has become your passion. Please tell us a little about it—how it has evolved and why you started it.

Collier

Angels Trace is not a good idea it is a God idea. I had a vision in 1995 after being disturbed over the brutal murder of Nicole Brown Simpson and the tragic killings of the two little boys of Susan Smith. I believe the justice system, the law enforcement agencies, the government, the communities, and the pastors let those families down. I prayed about it. Later, I had a dream. In this vision, I believe God instructed me to go around the world and help women. Little did I know at that time that I too would go through my own personal struggles and see my life seemingly fall to pieces.

Buoyed by an unwavering faith, tremendous courage, and the support and guidance of three amazing female mentors, I put my life back together one step at a time. I embarked on a new life of hope and found it. Remembering the dream I'd had a decade before, I decided to use my newfound wisdom and inspiring story of restoration and form Angels Trace in 2006.

Angels Trace is a faith-based, non-profit organization in Orlando that serves as a "lifeline" for single mothers and their children, many of them abused and homeless, struggling financially and emotionally because of divorce, family violence, unemployment, or lack of affordable housing. These single-parent families often have nowhere to turn. We coach them past all the drama in their lives and help shift these women toward a better future for their families. The single moms we work with are highly motivated individuals who are committed to living a life free of abuse and full of peace, joy, and independence.

Wright

You certainly are passionate about this. It appears that Angels Trace is in capable hands and will be serving as a "bridge over troubled waters" for lots of single mothers and their families now and for many years to come. What's it like seeing your dream come true?

Collier

I'm blown away! Angels Trace is a dream that I had the courage and faith to go after. I sent out a clarion call for people to join me. Dear friends and acquaintances immediately answered that call. Moved by my passion and concern for distressed single women and their children, they signed up to help. My vision was birthed.

An extraordinary network of volunteers rallied around me to support the mission of Angels Trace, which is to empower single mothers to make better choices for their families. It is marvelous to see so many people care for the welfare of others, and awesome to witness the bright smiles and tears of joy on the faces of the women and children we help.

While I realize I'm the face behind Angels Trace because I'm its founder, this organization is not about me. In fact, it's bigger than I am, and that's why I didn't name the foundation after me. Angels Trace is about providing a community of support to troubled single-parent families. I envision the organization will spread its wings and fly beyond my local Central Florida community. One of my sons or I will sit as Chairman of the Board of Directors of Angels Trace Foundation one day and marvel how dreams really do come true!

Wright

What a great conversation. I really do appreciate the time you've spent with me this afternoon to answer all these questions. I've learned a lot. I am very impressed with everything that you have accomplished. Your success is unbelievable and your effort to help better the lives of other people is commendable.

Collier

Thank you! It brings me a great deal of satisfaction. I just had a client speak at our annual fundraiser. This young single mother who was once homeless told my guests about how I have affected her life. She said, "I have found a life of independence thanks to Ms. Alice. Because of her support, I am now in my own apartment and on a path to achieve my goal to attend graduate school." I'm humbled, and of course thrilled, by her sentiments.

Wright

Today we have been talking with Alice Collier. She is a celebrated television news journalist. She has interviewed three United States Presidents as well as countless other celebrities. As we have found here today, her life has been full of impressive, great things and now all she does is help people. What a life!

Thank you, Alice, for being with us on *Success Strategies.*

Collier

You're welcome, David.

About Alice Collier

ALICE COLLIER is a multi-talented individual whose fame and success over the years transcends a variety of areas from television journalism to motivational speaking to non-profit charity work. A former award-winning television news anchor and talk show host who interviewed three U.S. Presidents, three U.S. Vice Presidents, and numerous celebrities over an illustrious fifteen-year career, Alice has gone on to establish herself as one of the country's premier motivational speakers and inspirational Life Coaches for women and professional women's groups. She's also the inspiration for Angels Trace, a unique, faith-based volunteer organization that serves as a lifeline of hope and support for single mothers and their families in crisis.

Alice Collier
Ms. Alice Omnimedia, Inc.
"Inspiring Women to Greatness"
P.O. Box 536951
Orlando, Florida 32853
407.228.6494
info@msalice.com
www.MsAlice.com

Chapter Twelve

An interview with…

Dr. Steven L. Anderson

Harness Your Passion

David Wright (Wright)

Today we're talking with Steve Anderson, founder of Integrated Leadership Systems (ILS), a consulting company that provides executive coaching, training, and organizational development. Some past clients include Honda of America, Worthington Industries, Nationwide, and Elmer's Products, Inc. Steve's passion is helping individuals become more effective leaders and assisting companies in creating world-class teams. Steve's eventual goal is to help ILS become the most sought-after leadership development organization in the world. He lives with his wife and children in Columbus, Ohio.

Steve, welcome to *Success Strategies!*

Steve Anderson (Anderson)

Thank you!

Wright

So how do you define success?

Anderson

Most people would define success as being rich, but I don't define it that way. I define success as one thing: happiness! When you think about money, you can get so single-minded in your pursuit of it that you leave everything else behind that allows you to remain successful. In fact, in the book *Think and Grow Rich,* Napoleon Hill talks about ten different kinds of riches, and money is the least important one. If you get all the other things right first, the money just takes care of itself. Money is a necessary, but not a sufficient ingredient in happiness. Warren Buffett, one of the two richest men in the world, said, "Success is being surrounded by people that love you." He said that by that definition half of the people on the Fortune 500 would be considered failures!

Wright

How does someone become successful?

Anderson

There are three things a person must do to become successful. The first is to determine their final objectives. Unfortunately, most people never do this. I think this is sad because if you do not know where you are going you will probably never get there. You will probably never achieve success without direction and focus.

Second, you should set short-term goals designed to achieve your long-term objectives. It is critical that you write these down and work on them daily. Keep them in a place where you will see them every day. As we all know it is very easy to get distracted from our goals. By writing them down we allow ourselves to stay focused.

Finally, you have to work to achieve balance between all of our lifelong objectives. It does you no good to become a millionaire, but ignore your family and your health while doing it. This is the most difficult part of the process.

Wright

How important is self-esteem to becoming successful?

Anderson

It is imperative. I believe that the most critical determining factor of your eventual success is believing that you're worth it! You have to have that feeling deep inside of yourself that "I want and deserve to be a successful human being!" And there's no way that a coach or any other person can give you that. Only you or your parents can give you that. In fact, Tom Peters in his book, *Passion for Excellence*, interviewed several hundred chief executive officers. He asked them about their childhoods and he described an eerily similar set of circumstances where the parents gave the children compliments and verbal support to the point of nausea. The child was just given this sense that "I am powerful and I can do whatever I want to do in my life." Once you have that, nothing can stop you!

Wright

What does success have to do with leadership?

Anderson

Everything. You can't become successful initially unless you lead, and you can't sustain success unless you continue to lead. So for instance, you may hitch your wagon to a star and ride on somebody else's coattails and become "successful" financially for a while, but you have to ultimately make up your mind that "I'm in charge of my own destiny." If you don't do that, in the long run someone else will control your destiny and you will not be happy or successful.

Wright

Who are the people who most heavily influenced your own success?

Anderson

There were six critical people in my life. The first one was my grandfather who was a tremendous leader and a man of great integrity; he loved his family deeply. He started a company in 1947 that now has 3,000 employees called The Andersons. He inspired me to become a great man someday and to learn how to lead just by his example.

The next people who were critical to my eventual success were my parents. I always knew that I was deeply loved as a child. They gave me the gift of self-esteem. This gift is probably the most critical ingredient in my success.

The fourth person was my Uncle Dick whom I was very close to as a child. I had a great deal of respect for him. He told me many times that I would make a difference in this world. This gave me the confidence that I could do whatever was necessary to achieve my dreams.

The fifth person was Dr. Henry Leuchter, a counselor I saw. He had a profound impact upon me. He showed me what it took to overcome my fears en route to making my dreams come true and becoming truly successful. He taught me how to care about other people's feelings, but not their approval. Learning this distinction was very important in my own development.

The last person and the most important person now is my wife, Char, who loves me unconditionally and makes me feel like the luckiest man on the planet every day. She has added a huge dose of humility and gentleness to the way I approach other people in relationships. Her influence has allowed me to become even more successful. She has also made my journey much more fun and rewarding.

Wright

What prevents most people from becoming more successful?

Anderson

I believe that fear prevents many people from becoming successful. There are two main emotions in our lives: fear and passion. If passion dominates our lives we will succeed. If fear dominates, we are doomed to failure. If we make up our minds we're going to harness our passion, there's nothing that can stop us from becoming successful. Sadly, 80 percent of human beings let fear dictate the long-term decisions in their life. When you let fear make your decisions for you, you start with a problem, which drives fear, which causes you to react. When you let passion run your life, you start with a vision, which drives your passion, which causes action! That's sustainable, and when you react to what's going on around you, that's *not* sustainable and will ultimately end in your own failure and unhappiness.

Wright

Must we serve other people in order to be successful?

Anderson

Yes. Up until now I have not talked about service, but service is absolutely critical to our long-term success. Zig Ziglar said, "You can get anything you want in life if you just help enough other people get the things they want in life!" And that's what I believe. There are three phases in our lives: learning, earning, and returning. And if you don't add this last piece, returning to humanity and the planet what you've taken from it as a child in terms of education and everything your parents have given you, you haven't completed your journey. As Stephen Covey said, "In order to have a great life and become happy and successful, you have to begin at the end." That is, you have to ask yourself, "What kind of legacy do I want to leave?" Start by writing that down. Then make a plan that explores the contribution you would have to make to leave that kind of legacy.

Wright

So how important is career choice in a person's success?

Anderson

It's absolutely critical. Sigmund Freud said, "To be happy, human beings have to do two things: love and work." The two most important decisions we make as human beings are who we choose for our life partner, and what we decide to do for our careers. If you work very hard at figuring out what it is that you were put here to do, and you try deeply to understand what's special about you and how you can best serve, you will never have to work another day in your life. So I get out of bed every morning excited because I get to make a difference for my clients doing something that I absolutely love to do. And that's what I find true of everybody who's ultimately successful—they absolutely love going to work.

Wright

I've got a lot of friends who have career choices to make, and if they have three choices they always go with the one that pays the most.

Anderson

That's a typical decision. I do a lot of executive coaching for people in similar types of situations, and when people want to choose that I say, "That's like my asking you why you're alive?" and you saying, "To breathe." While it's certainly important that you breathe, it's no reason to live. What you want to do if you want to find a good career is do something you love so much that you would do it for free—and you do it so well that people pay you to do it!

Wright

How did you decide on this career path?

Anderson

I never thought I would end up here, I can tell you that much. I feel like this career chose me, not the other way around. As I told you, when I was a child my family ran a very large business, and from the time I was ten years old I can remember being excited to work there someday. I got an agricultural business degree from Ohio State. I then followed a career path as a manager, but as I said earlier, I was in my twenties and struggling emotionally; things were just not clicking for me. At around age twenty-six I was really lost. That's when I sought counseling.

I went to see Dr. Leuchter, and to my surprise I loved being in therapy. I found it fascinating. When I was done with counseling I went to work for my family's business and I was very successful, but I was bored. I realized that what I wanted to do for other people was what Henry Leuchter did for me—help them make their lives great! At that time I went through a lot of soul-searching. I quit my job and earned a PhD in psychology. After graduate school I initially did clinical work, but eventually I decided to combine my business background and my master's degree in Business Administration with my PhD in Psychology to start Integrated Leadership Systems to help individuals and organizations actualize their potential.

Wright

How important do you think balance is in becoming successful?

Anderson

It is very important. Without balance success is not sustainable. I feel that too many young people focus all of their energy on financial success. When a person sacrifices everything for monetary gain they often end up burned out and lonely. These people usually arrive at middle age and say to themselves, "this is not working for me!" I know because that is what happened to me.

Now I put forth effort in several areas and I do my best to balance them all. In fact, I have three main goals for my life. The top one is to make my wife feel like a queen every day of her life. The second one is to be a great parent for my children, and the third one is to help my business to become the most sought-after leadership development organization in the world. And that's just the way it ought to be, in my opinion.

I also have to say that having a rich spiritual life is critical. That's how you keep your compass pointed true north all the time. Your priorities have to be spiritual life, then family, and then work if you want to have long-term sustainable success.

Wright

I had a life goal of being ninety, and I had a baby when I was fifty. She just went to college about four weeks ago so I'm up to one hundred!

Anderson

Good for you! How old are you, David?

Wright

Sixty-eight.

Anderson

That's so neat. I think that planning on a long life makes the journey so much more interesting. I just turned fifty on June 7, so I figure I'm halfway done. I was running a half marathon last winter and I passed this other runner. I start talking to him and found out that he has run 250 marathons, one in every state in the United States five times, and he's seventy years old. It was just absolutely a humbling experience to be in his presence!

Wright

I went to one of my friend's birthday parties last evening, and he's going on a twenty-five mile hike in the Smoky Mountains; he's seventy.

Many of us who have been working for quite some time intellectually understand balance (and when you have a baby at fifty you're forced into a little bit of balance). Why do you think most people abuse balance so much?

Anderson

I think our society is obsessed with success—not in the sense of happiness, I mean money. We love the winner. We think that if we're not producing, we're not worthwhile.

I learned when I was in counseling that you have to spend a part of your life on the balcony, not on the dance floor. If you're always on the dance floor you can't really see the pattern of your life. If you dedicate a part of every week to looking at the process of your life, you will be able to easily eliminate activities that do not contribute to your overall happiness. When you take time to evaluate your life, you inevitably realize that your time here is very short and you have to use every minute wisely. To use an analogy of driving, many people have their noses pressed to the windshield and they're driving ninety miles an hour down the freeway with no idea what highway they're on or what their ultimate destination is. They don't realize that they're almost out of gas and oil.

My advice is to sit back in your seat, take a rest stop before you start your trip, and ask yourself, "Where am I going?" Then sit back in your seat while you're driving and scan the dashboard and check to make sure you are on the right road. Pay attention—don't just look at where you're going—pay attention to your overall journey. Is it going all right? Ask yourself, "Do I need maintenance? Do I need to stop?"

Balance is very difficult to achieve, but it is worth the effort. It is also important to understand that you are never done working on balance. It is a never-ending battle and it is hard work.

Wright

It's very difficult when you're in business to get this balance thing. The last four years I've been going to the beach and walking two and three hours a morning on the beach. Every year I've been promising myself I would come home and continue that routine; I never did until now. I made that decision the second week in July to come home to the beach, and I haven't missed a day yet. I feel much better, and I'm also spending more time doing other things—balance leads to more balance!

Anderson

You're right. It's like success begets success, and it's like money in the bank account, "That feels pretty good! It works; I'm going to keep on doing that!" I can tell you, when I first started getting on the balcony and looking at my life and spending that quiet time, I felt really guilty. I really struggled with it for five years, but then just as you did, David, eventually I just started saying, "This really works!" What I noticed was that very few people around me were as happy as I was or as successful as I was.

Another great leader, John Maxwell, says he has "a thinking chair." He goes and sits in it, and he said if he stays away from it too long it starts calling his name out, "Hey! Get over here! Sit down! Be quiet!" Also, S. Truett Cathy, the chief executive officer of Chick-Fil-A goes to a cabin he owns every ninety days with just a blank pad of paper, the whole day. He says that by being quiet he gets the necessary insights to grow his business. And Chick-Fil-A is the fastest growing fast food chain in the United States. He's eighty, and he's still the chief executive officer of that company. I think that taking time to get on the balcony is critical to achieving balance and long-term success.

Wright

I talked to him a few months ago and he's phenomenal. It addition to that, he's put hundreds of kids through college. I think he said he lost hundreds of million dollars by closing on Sunday, but he decided he's going to close on Sunday.

Anderson

And that's balance—that's putting values ahead of profits! And he makes as much money in six days as the other companies make in seven days. You might think it's a bad decision to be closed for business part of the time. In my organization we don't see clients on Friday, generally, unless somebody has an emergency. And you would guess that we are going to make 20 percent less than our competitors, but I believe that having Fridays to plan for the upcoming week and develop our team makes us more effective. You have to take care of yourself and your employees if you are going to achieve ultimate success.

Wright

This has been a great conversation, Steve. I really do appreciate all this time you've taking with me today answering all these questions.

About Steve Anderson

DR. STEVE ANDERSON received his Bachelor of Science in Agriculture from Ohio State University in 1980. From 1980 until 1994 he held several management positions in the agriculture and retail industries. During this time he obtained his master's in Business Administration from Capital University in Columbus, Ohio. In 1999 he earned his PhD in psychology at the Ohio State University. After graduating he worked as a counselor and sports psychologist at Denison University. Since 2001 he has run his consulting company, Integrated Leadership Systems, which does leadership training, motivational speaking, executive coaching, and organizational development for companies in Ohio and the surrounding areas. He is a columnist for *Columbus Business First* and author of two books, *The Call to Authenticity* and *Embracing Rebellion*.

Steve Anderson, PhD, MBA
President and Senior Consultant
Integrated Leadership Systems, LLC
3805 N. High St., Suite 310
Columbus, OH 43214
614.784.8530
steve@integratedleader.com
www.integratedleader.com

Chapter Thirteen

An interview with...

Marjorie Blanchard

Attaining Success in Business & Life

David Wright (Wright)

Today we're talking with Marjorie Blanchard. Ms. Blanchard has earned a reputation worldwide as a compelling motivational speaker, accomplished management consultant and trainer, best-selling author, and entrepreneur. In 1983 she was chosen Speaker of the Year by *New Women* magazine and American Express. She was co-recipient, along with her husband, Dr. Kenneth Blanchard, of the *1991 Entrepreneur of the Year Award* from Cornell University.

She is co-author of *The One Minute Manager Gets Fit* and *Working Well: Managing for Health and High Performance*. Marjorie is well versed in a variety of topics and often speaks on leadership and empowerment, team building, customer service, managing change, and life planning.

As co-founder of Blanchard Training and Development Inc., she has worked diligently with her husband in developing the company into one of the premier management consulting and training companies in the world. She served as president of the company from 1987 to 1997, leading its rapid growth and success. She now heads the firm's unique Office of the Future—a think tank charged with shaping the future of both the training industry and the company.

It's my pleasure to welcome Marjorie to *Success Strategies*. Thank you for being with us.

Marjorie Blanchard (Blanchard)

I'm delighted to be here.

Wright

Before we dig into some specifics relating to success in business and life, I know our readers would appreciate a little background information about you. I'm always curious about the life journey of our special guests and their early influences, experiences, mentors, and such. Will you tell us a little about your background?

Blanchard

Well, even though we have lived in California for about twenty-five years now, I was raised on the East Coast. I was born in Rochester, New York, the oldest in a family of five—four girls and one boy. My brother is eighteen years younger and actually, he's replaced me as president of our company. I'm right now the head of the "Office of the Future," which is a wonderful job for me. Tom and I are the bookends of this family.

My mom and dad met at Cornell, where I also went to school and where I met my husband. I'd say that the biggest early influence, in addition to being the oldest sibling in the family and having young sisters and a brother to feel responsible for, was that we moved quite a bit. My dad worked in the meat packing business and in order to progress and work his way up, we moved about every three years. That was quite a remarkable experience as I look back on it. I didn't necessarily like it when it was happening, but what it did was make me feel very close to my family—my major reference group.

Another big influence, I would say, was when I was about six. My parents bought a piece of property on one of the Finger Lakes. Throughout my whole growing-up years we would spend the summer camping out there. I think that made me pretty close to my family. We had some marvelous times enjoying everything from camping out to evenings without television, a lot of good reading time, time alone, and just a lot of family time. Ken and I committed to that when we got married.

I married right out of college and had a wonderful experience at Cornell. We spent about ten years in the academic world and then Ken was eligible for a sabbatical. We came to California, discovered this amazing climate, and decided to stay here. Two or three years later we started our company—Blanchard Training and Development—now the Ken Blanchard Company. We just celebrated our twenty-fifth anniversary in the company. Ken and I have been married forty-two years.

Wright

Oh my! That's odd in this culture.

Blanchard

I keep thinking someone is going to come and interview me about that. We have two children, both in their thirties, and two grandchildren. Our daughter and son both work in our company. In fact, we're transitioning the leadership of the company to them. We have about three hundred people in the company right now and they're spread across the country and the world.

Wright

That would be a great book title—*How to Stay Married*.

Blanchard

It would be, wouldn't it?

Wright

You couldn't say anything about "one minute" in it—that would be for sure.

Blanchard

Somebody did do a study of married people. In order to get a population that was big enough, he had to get down to people who somewhat liked each other and decided to stay married.

Wright

I've got to hear more about this. I've never heard of a "company of the future." What in the world is that all about? It sounds like I want to go to work for you.

Blanchard

It's a wonderful thing.

Wright

What do you do in the Company of the Future?

Blanchard

Well, what happened was in 1997, I was very much up to my ears with being president and getting very frustrated because there was so much happening in our industry regarding technology—e-learning, the whole boom in the dot com business, and the Internet. I just had this growing stack of articles to read and conferences I wanted to go to and things we needed to do research on because we could see the age of technology looming on the horizon. We had a wonderful year that year and I petitioned our family to create this "office of the future," which would consist of five people in a little think-tank. Our goal was to get smart on some of these issues we didn't know very much about, to study the trends and the literature, and to prepare our company for some big changes.

We started some experiments with distance learning within the company. We also protected a relationship we had with the company that was putting some of our core intellectual property from our books onto very, very interesting interactive programs.

Then when 9/11 came along and our clients couldn't or wouldn't travel, we were ready. We actually had alternatives to classroom training. What we're now doing is more of a blended approach where people learn a lot more before they get to class so that when they're in class they get to practice and really apply what they're learning to their very own situation. It was a godsend, honestly, because we had previously done a lot of talking but not a lot of doing in that area.

We did a big international study—a lot of our international business is growing—and we were able to spend about four months studying about twenty-eight countries, looking at what some of the opportunities were. We're still doing a lot of pushing in the company to get them to use existing technology and much less future technology. We continue to work on these study topics by doing trend watches, scenario planning, and all the things the smallest companies are too busy to do. Most businesses are so busy with the present they ignore the future and then get surprised.

Wright

As you work with organizations across America, are there one or two issues that seem to stand out above the rest—areas of concern for corporate leaders? For example, are leadership problems occupying most of your attention or perhaps change managing and cultural issues?

Blanchard

Well, I think all of those are huge issues. Our core technology is in the leadership area, both on a platform for volunteer organizations and in corporate America.

I have recently been looking very carefully at the retention issue. There are some very clear signs we could have a big labor shortage in the United States, certainly by the year 2010, that will make what we experience in the late '90s look minor. So what I'm encouraging people and our clients to do is, first of all, take that issue seriously. Start looking at your own retention figures and where you might be losing people you want to keep and that kind of thing.

One of the reasons people leave an organization is because they don't like the way they see people being treated or they don't feel they are developing in their career. It almost always boils down to the fact that they don't have a very good relationship with their manager or leader. They don't feel they're being coached or nurtured or given enough attention. What I'm warning and encouraging managers and leaders to do, through white papers and other methods, is to make sure people feel like they're in a culture where it's a great place to work and where they would recommend their friends to come and work. You can't start doing that when the chips are down—you've got to do it all along the way.

Almost all of Ken's writings have to do with honoring people, paying attention to them one by one—not as a group necessarily—and understanding that your people are your main competitive advantage; you really do get back what you give to people in terms of loyalty, etc.

Wright

Don't you wish more corporate presidents would talk the way you do?

Blanchard

You know, some do, but what they don't know is how to go from where they are now to a culture they want to have. Sometimes they start by reading the books we've written and they get excited and inspired. Maybe they have one of our speakers come in or Ken will come in and hold a workshop or one of our speakers will speak during a meeting to get them excited about how things can be different. Then it becomes a series of things they put in place to act on their good intentions. Most of the companies we work with are great companies already; they just want to get better.

Wright

I was in intrigued by the titles of your books. Both of them focus on health and wellness in the workplace—*The One Minute Manager Gets Fit* and *Working Well: Managing for Health and High Performance*. First, how did you find yourself writing on the topic of health in the workplace?

Blanchard

I was a little ahead of myself. Those books actually came out in the 1980s, around 1986 or 1987. I became very interested in this whole idea of whether a manager can make someone sick. What we found was, we would talk with somebody one time and they'd be fine and when we talked with him or her two or three months later, the person would be ill or missing work or hating life or whatever. What we'd find is these people had gotten a new manager.

In the book *Working Well*, Dr. Mark Tager—a physician with a very holistic approach—and I went around asking questions like, "What do managers do that makes people sick?" and, "How can you create a culture where that's not happening?" It was that area we really started focusing in on. We wanted to know just how important managers are to the people who report to them and to those who depend on them. We wanted to know what to do to convince them they can do a lot in this area and they are very, very important. That was the beginning of that whole thing.

Negative relationships between managers and employees really do show up in absenteeism. You can keep your job pretty much with 20 percent of your energy. You can also give a 100 percent of your energy. We continue to look at that gap between 20 percent and 100 percent, saying that's really where a company's competitive advantage is.

You go into Starbucks and you know those people are turned on; they really like what they're doing and they're giving good service. It's because they know they're treated well and they're growing, etc.

Wright

I'd love to dig a little deeper if you don't mind. Were there some specifics you discussed with people in these managing jobs? Did you give them any advice about what they could do to not make people sick?

Blanchard

I think the biggest piece of advice I would give to managers, and probably to parents and spouses also, is that you need to spend one-on-one time with the people on whom you depend and who report to you. Now, what I encourage managers to do is to set aside fifteen to thirty minutes once a week or at a minimum, once every two weeks to have a one-on-one meeting individually with the people who report to them. The unique thing about this meeting is it's not another little mini-performance status check. It's really a meeting to talk about what's on the mind of the people who report to you.

The meeting will start out with the manager asking, "What's on your mind?" So it's a responsibility of the manager to have the meeting and commit to it, make sure that it's a top priority, and that it happens consistently. It's really the responsibility of the direct report to bring the issues.

I've been doing this now for a number of years and you'd be amazed at what's on people's minds that have to do with their own career or they may be concerned about an aging parent problem or maybe they've heard something through the company grapevine that needs some kind of clarification. Just the fact that somebody will take the time and honor that time to provide the communication infrastructure so many organizations want and don't have is important to employees. It gets rid of any feelings of alienation and isolation very prevalent in a lot of organizations—you need a touch-point in an organization.

I think it works just the same at home—having one-on-one time with each one of your children, even if it's once every other week for a half hour. What I've found with my own people is that they save up things. They come in and I ask, "What's on your mind?" They've got a little list of things they want to talk about because they know that the time they have with me is protected. It's not an interruption and it actually saves me time because they aren't interrupting me while I'm doing something else. They know they're going to have that focused and concentrated time. This is just one of the things we try to keep in place.

When we do leadership training we state that this training will only come alive if you make sure you create a place for people to have this connection—that's so meaningful. That information is being proven in so many of the retention studies—people don't leave companies, they leave managers. People don't leave marriages, they leave spouses. There is a need we have to connect. If there's one thing people could do it would be to rely less on group meetings and to make sure you have these one-on-one meetings.

Wright

In your experience do you think the employee knows it is a confidential time as well?

Blanchard

Well, it usually is, and you certainly set up the rules for that. You can decide how you want to make that work. What people appreciate more than anything is your time. Now, I would say initially, it can be a little awkward if you've not done that before. We give people questions like, "What's going on in your job that I might not know about?" We get things going at first, but after awhile even the shyest will take the opportunity and feel comfortable talking to their managers.

I got this idea from a fellow who was running three Wienersnitzel restaurant franchises. His three restaurants had a remarkably low turnover, both in the management staff and in the frontline staff. When I talked with him, he said the only thing he was doing differently was requiring the store manager to meet individually with the teenagers who were working for them, fifteen minutes once a week. It took these managers three and a half hours once a week to meet with these employees. Why would any of these employees go down the street for fifty cents more an hour if somebody's taking an interest in them, particularly at that age where it may be their first job? They appreciate somebody on a consistent level making time for them.

Wright

Marjorie, you and your husband, Ken, were awarded "Entrepreneur of the Year" back in 1991. Many of our readers are either thinking about striking out on their own or they're in the middle of a turbulent entrepreneurial adventure. First, what are your feelings about entrepreneurs in general, and secondly, will you address one or two big picture issues that most entrepreneurs face and struggle with?

Blanchard

Having been an entrepreneur, frankly I think entrepreneurship is a mixed blessing. I remember reading a book called the *Entrepreneurial Woman* by Sandra Winston, years ago. It was refreshing to see in print some of the things I had experienced.

One of the things she said was that very often, entrepreneurs become entrepreneurs because of some disruptive event. I call them "cosmic boosts"—something that shakes them out of their comfort zone like getting fired or having some kind of tragedy happen at home where they need to make more money or something that gives them energy. Cosmic boosts are important because you need energy if you're going to be an entrepreneur. You'll need a lot of independent energy and you'll have to keep that energy going on your own. You generally don't have somebody coaching you, so you'll need to have a boost into this new world.

Sometimes a cosmic boost is as simple as feeling like you aren't going to make progress in this bigger organization and now's the time. You obviously need to have the resources and you need to know what the business is. For example, sometimes I suggest to people that if they are going to think about starting their own travel agency, maybe they ought to work for somebody who has experience in that area of expertise for a while—get to know the ropes before going into a brand new venture without really knowing about it.

Entrepreneurs have to be very independent. I think you need to be able to pat yourself on the back and take responsibility for what's good and bad and not rely on other people.

I think there are some characteristics of successful entrepreneurs. Often, people who are successful entrepreneurs had parents, grandparents, or other relatives who where entrepreneurs, so they were able to see what it was like to be in an independent situation like that.

In many ways there's a lot of freedom but then there's also a lot of responsibility that comes with it. I don't think entrepreneurship is the only way to be successful in life. I think you can be successful within a larger organization if you are clear about how you're going to save the money you make, etc.

There are periods of time in a person's life when being an entrepreneur may not be the best choice if there are mouths to feed and heavy monetary responsibilities.

You can also see some tremendous successes. I started as an entrepreneur with a partner and one of the things I learned was that having a partner was a bit like getting married—I had to figure out how we were going to work together. There are also a lot of wonderful joys that come with it. You're pretty much responsible for yourselves and if you hit on a good idea and can figure it out, you can always get a good group of advisors. You can do some wonderful things. I heard someone say only about 7 percent of businesses make it to twenty-five years; we recently celebrated our twenty-fifth company anniversary. It's not a walk in the park, but it can be successful.

Wright

Regarding the "cosmic boost" you were talking about, I was fairly successful in business one time. I went to $40 million in about five years, which would be about $150 million today. Everybody says, "Boy that's great! You must have had a good plan." If they only knew. I started working for this company and I thought the owner of the company was an idiot. So I thought I would change companies. I changed to another one—a bigger and better one that I thought would be bigger and better, but that owner turned out to be an even bigger idiot, so I started looking around. I loved the industry, but people who were mistreating their employees headed all the companies. So I just opened my own business.

Blanchard

That's a good cosmic boost, but at least you knew the business and knew what it took, that's important. I do believe you do need to know the business. In our own company, we were out of business a few times and didn't even know it. So there are stages when you're growing that can get you in trouble—you get over-extended or you're *too* successful. We put out a four-color catalogue one time and we almost drowned in the response because we really didn't know what was going to happen. I look back at several points in the history of our company when God was definitely watching over us—we were very blessed to survive.

Wright

Many of our clients are pursuing success at many levels in their careers, in relationships, and concerning their health. I know you do quite a bit of personal development consulting and life planning. Will you share with our readers some advice that may address some of the more bedrock fundamental principles we all deal with in our pursuit of success?

Blanchard

I think my biggest advice probably goes back to moderation. I have known many people who've worked very hard to be successful. They've finally reached the pinnacle of success only to find they've probably lost their most significant relationships and lost their health as well. I think young people see that more clearly than even our generation. They are already asking questions about balance. It is necessary to continue to consider how you can keep nurturing the things that are truly the most important—your health and your relationships—while you're on your journey to success. You can maybe work really hard for a few months, but if you just keep the burner turned up all the time, something's going to give.

In the case of our relationship, Ken and I made some decisions about things we would and wouldn't do. For example, we decided we would make every effort in the world to be together on weekends even though Ken does a lot of traveling and I was traveling for a while. That sometimes meant flying home on Friday night and leaving Sunday afternoon, but it was a commitment we made. We have a summer cottage at Skaneateles that was used by my family during our get-togethers. Ken and I made time for each other to go there in the summer.

It's amazing—if you put your own goals out there, other people's lives will fit around them. If you don't have goals about setting aside time for your family, then you get ticked off by all those other folks who interfere with that. You need to be stubborn. We have some rituals and some blocks of time that we really protect; when we don't protect them we feel pretty badly about it. It took us a while to see where those real stresses were; but I think you need to put that little bit of structure in.

I love the idea of "date night." We didn't have this when Ken and I were first married. I just think that's the coolest idea. What it indicates is that a couple is going to put their relationship, at least for one night a week, ahead of everything else. They're going to get a babysitter and they're going to spend some time talking together or going to a movie or doing whatever. What it shows is they're committed to that primary relationship ahead of a lot of the other things taking their time.

This refers back to redefining balance for yourself, not so much as structuring a strict nine-to-five, but in regards to establishing those priority areas and making your schedule reflect those things you determine are important.

It's the same with health. I've walked now for years out on the golf course with two other women. Just knowing they're waiting for me, even if I get back at night, gets me up and going at six in the morning. They give me support and some structure for my good intentions. I think that's kept me balanced over a long, long period of time. You'd think by now I'd be totally self-sufficient but I'll tell you, if those ladies weren't involved, I might not be getting up. I went this morning even though I was out late last night. First of all it is fun—we complain about how we feel, we solve the problems of the world, and we talk about how great we're going to look when we're seventy-five. It might be hard to get my clothes on and get out there, but my persistence shows I'm acting on my good intentions.

Wright

It sounds to me like you don't make a whole lot of short-term plans. Regarding the cottage you and Ken go to, did you go there as a child?

Blanchard

I did. It was our touchstone. Eventually Ken and I bought a cottage near my parents' cottage. We're now fortunate to be able to spend nine weeks there because we've transferred a lot of our leadership responsibilities here. Our children love to come too and they want to bring their children. So it's one of those things that has been a nice balance for our busy schedule.

Wright

I have a warm feeling just thinking about all the memories that must be running around that cottage after all these years, going all the way back to your childhood.

Blanchard

The biggest thing we decided was not to have television there.

Wright

Is that right?

Blanchard

We have never had television up there. I'll tell you, when our children were teenagers they would complain saying things like, oh, the Olympics this, and what about the soap opera? I would tell them they could walk over to their grandmother's and watch it; but we've never had television there. Now the children come up and it's the first thing they tell their friends. They puff up a little and say, "Well, we've never had television here." It causes us to have more time together to play games, have campfires, and pay attention to each other on a different level than we do at home.

Wright

That is a wonderful thought. Before we wrap up today, do you have any final thoughts for our readers? Will you share with us any information about up-coming books or incentives you're working on?

Blanchard

I think that one of the most interesting trends I'm following is this idea of "spirit at work and spirit at home." I really believe people want to lead at a higher level. They really want to believe their lives are making a difference. They really do want to work for an organization that they sense either lives by its values or is committed to some portion of the common good. Perhaps it even has some kind of religious connection. I believe that when we hear people—especially young people—talking about "meaningful work," they're expressing a desire to be part of something bigger and to have something that gives extra energy. I believe that that takes thinking.

One of Ken's books is called *Gung Ho*. The first secret of *Gung Ho* is meaningful work—how what you're doing is connected to what's beneficial to the organization, good for society, and helpful for the common good. I think that's also something families should spend time talking about.

We need to be asking questions like what is it that's bigger than we are? What are the volunteer things we're going to do or how are we going to make the world a better place? That kind of energy I think will sustain us though what I believe is a tremendous barrage of bad news in the media. We really have to work on keeping our spirits up. We have to be with other spirit-minded people, and I also think we have to realize that the only reason the media does well is because they report bad news. You have to be careful as a manager or as a parent not to let yourself to begin to think that the world is changing and people just aren't as good as they used to be.

As a manager I remember that bad news rises and personal victories stay hidden. You've got to go looking for those personal victories and focus on what's good. You have to keep yourself inspired.

If I had any advice it would be to encourage people to understand that they need to focus on the bigger picture in their lives. They need to know where they're headed and what's important; then they need to spend some time each day remembering that. Some people accomplish this with prayer, some with meditation. Whatever method you use, I think you have to recalibrate every day because there's so much out there threatening to drag you down.

Leadership, I think, is about going somewhere and it's about creating an exciting look at where you're going; then people want to follow you. That happens at home and I believe it also happens in the office. It can happen in your own department, it doesn't always have to come from the top.

Wright

What a wonderful conversation. You sound like one of the most thoughtful and levelheaded women I've ever talked with.

Blanchard

That comes from being in your sixties, right?

Wright

Yes, it does!

We've been speaking today with Marjorie Blanchard, best-selling author, speaker, management consultant, and entrepreneur.

Marjorie, thank you so much for being with us.

Blanchard

Well, it was a pleasure.

About Marjorie Blanchard

DR. MARJORIE BLANCHARD has earned a reputation worldwide as a compelling motivational speaker, an accomplished management consultant and trainer, a best-selling author, and an entrepreneur. She was chosen as Speaker of the Year by *New Woman* magazine and American Express. She was also co-recipient—with her husband, Ken Blanchard—of the 1991 Entrepreneur of the Year award from Cornell University.

Co-author of *The One Minute Manager Gets Fit* and *Working Well: Managing for Health and High Performance*, Marjorie is well versed on a variety of topics. She often speaks on leadership, balance, managing change, aging parents, and life planning.

As co-founder of Blanchard Training and Development Inc., she has worked diligently with her husband in developing the company into one of the premier management consulting and training companies in the world. She served as president of the company from 1987 to 1997, leading its rapid growth and success. She now heads the firm's unique Office of the Future—a think tank charged with shaping the future of both the training industry and the company.

Marjorie received both her bachelor's and master's degrees from Cornell University and her doctorate from the University of Massachusetts, Amherst.

Chapter Fourteen

An interview with...

Dianne Hofner Saphiere & Kathleen A. Curran

Intercultural Business Effectiveness

David Wright (Wright)

Today we're talking with Dianne Hofner Saphiere and Kathleen A. Curran.

Dianne brings a wealth of global business experience to her consulting practice, specializing in improving her clients' intercultural management performance. She has managed multinational, virtual project teams since 1989. She speaks Japanese, Spanish, and English, and has lived one-third of her life outside the United States on three different continents. Her direct business experience has been in marketing alcoholic beverages and running a global consulting services organization. Her key clients have been in the electronics, energy, financial services, hospitality, manufacturing, and specialty chemical industries. Dianne is a frequent author, a twenty-plus-year faculty member of the Intercultural Communication Institute, and a recipient of the International Society for Intercultural Education, Training and Research's (SIETAR) Outstanding Interculturalist award.

Kathleen is an intercultural business coach and trainer who is passionate about cultivating in her clients strategies for achieving business objectives across cultures, and building a truly global organizational mindset and practical, supportive systems. She has lived and worked in Asia for over twenty years, and is the principal of Intercultural Systems, a global intercultural consulting, training, and coaching firm founded in Singapore in 1996. The firm serves government agencies, educational institutions, and Global 500 corporations through offices in Singapore and Houston, Texas. She is co-author of *Cultural Detective®: Singapore* and *Cultural Detective®: Malaysia* and is actively involved in intercultural dialogue on the community level through the Society for Intercultural Education, Training, and Research.

Dianne and Kathleen, welcome to *Success Strategies!*

Dianne Saphiere (Saphiere) & Kathleen Curran (Curran)

Thank you very much, David.

Wright

When we meet a dentist, a lawyer, even an executive coach, most of us have a clear understanding of what that person does for a living; but "intercultural consultant?" I can only imagine the explanations you have to get into at a cocktail party! Can you tell us a bit about what it is that you do?

Saphiere

Yes, we get that question a lot! For years, my mother actually told people I was an interpreter! Basically, what we do is help people work together more productively and enjoyably in international and multicultural environments. Say a group of people on different continents manage a product line; they might only see each other a few times a year, yet they need to agree on how they are going to share information and make decisions. Somebody in an intercultural consultant role like Kathleen or myself will help them to be able to hear each other, understand the differing perspectives they each bring to the table, and help them as a team develop work processes that will function for them and enable them to utilize all their skills more fully.

Curran

Also, through training, coaching, and consulting with individual executives, teams, and work groups, we help develop the personal attitudes, perspectives, and skills for collaborating effectively across cultures in order to achieve their key objectives and results. We then work with organizations to make sure that their structures and systems support and reward the development of those new competencies.

We often work in the international arena, but we want to emphasize that culture goes beyond the passport level. We use Ed Schein's definition of culture that he introduced years ago—a culture is a group of people who share rules about "how we do things around here." So *culture* can actually refer to many levels of culture: organizational culture, business unit, profession (we've all experienced the differences between HR, engineering or IT), team culture as well as ethnicity, gender, spiritual traditions, and so on.

A big part of what we do involves turning on light bulbs so that people can see the various culturally-influenced perspectives that they may be working with, realize the impact of their own cultural sense, and become aware of their own lenses or ways of looking at the world, plus explore how their customers and colleagues may be doing the same. So while intercultural is less well known as a field than engineering, what we do enables our clients to create and implement their own and their organizations' success strategies across cultures.

Wright

Are you saying that even in my company, which only has maybe twenty people working here in this building, there are different cultures?

Saphiere

You bet there are, David. I'm sure your staff members are different ages and genders. They probably have different socio-economic levels, perhaps different sexual orientations, and there may even be different nationalities and ethnicities in the group—those are all cultures.

Wright

Who are your primary customers, and why do they come to you?

Curran

Our clients come to us for a wide range of issues. On the broad systemic level, organizations may want to look at their policies or initiatives that need to be rolled out and implemented on a global basis. Sometimes teams or work groups comprised of people from many cultures want to enhance their collaboration and communication effectiveness. A third level is the individual executives who want to improve the effectiveness of their leadership skills across cultures.

I think the best way to explain is by example. A large U.S. logistics company once came to us with a puzzle. They had a great promotion-from-within policy, but almost no one in Southeast Asia was applying for the available promotions. Their future management pool would be quite shallow if more applicants didn't participate. So the questions were, 1) is there a cultural reason behind this, and 2) how can we implement this policy more culturally effectively for greater success?

Saphiere

Regarding your question about whether this applies to a company like yours, we had a very interesting non-international project a couple of years ago. It was a request from a large semiconductor firm. They needed to save major money by streamlining operations. They basically wanted to combine four different divisions into one, getting rid of three of their division heads and a lot of redundancies. They hired us to come in as cross-culturalists, and even though they were all U.S.-based people, they definitely had the different silos of their divisions; the competition and the backstabbing between these four division heads was just incredible.

Another example I can think of to illustrate the kind of customers we work with is on a more tactical level. We've worked for years with one of the world's largest energy companies. They want their employees worldwide to collaborate effectively with other employees in other locations around the world, and of course they're all working by phone and by e-mail, but none of these people has ever really been prepared to work virtually. So they wanted us to help them create a cross-cultural business skills development program that they could roll out anywhere in the world.

A project I'm working on right now, that is really fascinating for me because I've done so much international work, is in Los Angeles in a manufacturing environment. For me it's unique because the plant management in L.A. is primarily Latino. The workers are Latino and African-American, and their head office, made up of all Anglo-Americans, is located in the Midwest. Talk about needing to have a flexible communication style to succeed in that environment!

Curran

On the individual level, we also coach executives who are relocating to live and work in new cultures. For example, one gentleman from South America I worked with requested coaching to help him really take advantage of the international experience his expatriate assignment provided. Global coaching helped him not only to become a more effective global leader, but also to capture and articulate those specific skills and learning that he could develop and reinvest in his organization—significant ROI for both him and his company!

This was a fantastic as well as visionary request, because so often we take for granted what we've learned to do, especially when we're in the fast-paced and demanding international environment. And in any expatriate assignment, there's the extra stress of really wanting to perform while simultaneously needing to quickly adjust to the culture we've moved to. As a result, when asked later, we can't always articulate what we learned, how we learned it, what worked, or what didn't.

The South American executive, for example, is very good at building cohesiveness on his very diverse multicultural team. But how does he do it? What personal best practice can he identify and take with him? When he returns to South America and his boss asks him, "How was the United States?" he wants to have concrete examples to illustrate his global leadership skills that can contribute to his further advancement in the organization. Enabling one to meet both career and personal objectives on the expatriate assignment is another way we work with our clients to help them really take advantage of their international experience and develop impactful success strategies.

Wright

Both of you speak with real passion about intercultural effectiveness. How did you become involved in this work? And what skills and experience do each of you bring?

Saphiere

Yes, passion for intercultural effectiveness is something we share. Kathleen and I both have worked internationally and interculturally for decades. I grew up out in the Southwestern United States with the Hopi, Navajo, and Latino communities, then I lived for quite a while in Mexico, Spain, and Japan. I've also worked throughout Western Europe. Kathleen has worked throughout Southeast Asia and with the Saudi government. We've both worked in the business world for a long time, so we've lived the difficulties and experienced the challenges of running a business on a global basis, which is vital for relating to our client's situations and needs.

In addition to our life experiences, it is important that we both have advanced degrees in the field. Mine are in Organizational and Human Resource Development and International Studies. Kathleen has her advanced degree in Intercultural Communication and credentials in executive coaching. We realized early on that having traveled to or worked in a particular culture is not sufficient qualification to advise somebody else how to do business there.

Therefore, what we bring to our clients is the practical business experience, a rigorous academic and professional background, and process skills and tools to help transform how they work together. This combination makes us much better able to connect with our clients and facilitate their intercultural success.

Wright

Globalization seems to be evident in nearly every aspect of our lives. Most people live in diverse communities, have international neighbors or friends, work in multinational and multicultural teams, and talk with outsourced sales or support reps, yet most of us have not received an education or had the opportunity to develop skills for working cross-culturally. What are some of the most important things for us to know?

Saphiere

It really is remarkable how multinational everything is these days. It's only recently that more and more people in every walk of life are communicating across cultures in their everyday work. Even local facilities in the heartland of America often have staff members from twenty or more different countries. And it's not just at work; all of us go to the dry cleaner, we visit the bank, attend a PTA meeting—everywhere we look we find diversity! Our schools and hospitals deal with speakers of dozens of different languages. We're living in communities that are multi-racial and multi-ethnic; they include multiple spiritual traditions and nationalities. We really feel that everybody needs the ability to communicate effectively across cultures if we want to succeed, whether it's in our work or our daily life.

Curran

Communicating effectively across cultures is especially challenging because just as you highlighted in your question, most have never really received any intercultural education.

Let me describe our natural perceptual process and show how powerful it is! Basically, we see something—an action, an object—and we try to make sense of it based on what we already know or are familiar with. Then in a split second, usually unconsciously, we evaluate whether we agree or not, like it or not, or think that action is right or wrong.

A very simple example of this process that I recall occurred when I first moved to Malaysia. I was in the market looking at all the prepared food on display. In one dish I saw carrots, potatoes, gravy, clearly a kind of stew—but what's that? Chicken feet! I spent very little time mentally trying to describe objectively what I saw or even trying to interpret that maybe chicken feet are a kind of food that someone else enjoys. My immediate reaction was negative, "Feet? Who eats the feet! We throw that part away!" I very quickly evaluated this dish negatively, according to my own cultural norms. Our perceptions are so powerful that if I took this example further, I could decide that I don't like Malaysian food, that Malaysians eat strange things, or that I will only go to McDonald's! So my very simple perception can lead to a change in my attitude and, based on this very limited experience, produce a negative stereotype about millions of people and their way of life, and even effect a change in my behavior and future decisions.

Now that example of the process of perception may be a funny one, but if we put this same process in the work context, you can imagine the repercussions. Let's say that my colleague did not reply to my e-mail within a couple of days. If I feel that e-mails should be responded to quickly, I may feel that my colleague is really inefficient and perhaps even that he is lacking in competence. My negative evaluation could influence my perceptions and attitudes in the future. I may think, "Oh, people from 'that culture' are so slow; they don't have that sense of urgency we need in business." So when a future opportunity arises to work for another team with colleagues from that particular culture, I may think, "Uh oh, this is going to be difficult." That simple perception from one limited experience may negatively influence my attitude and behavior rather unfairly. This shows that our reliance on our assumptions, misperceptions, and misinterpretations can be very damaging to effective working relationships.

One very important lesson that I've learned is that any time another person's action gets our attention, which is usually because it's contrary to what we expect and believe is correct, stop and reflect on it. Ask yourself, "What about that action affected me as it did?" Was it that someone was too slow in responding, too direct in their communication? Usually an action gets our attention because we value the opposite. We may value more speed and efficiency or more diplomacy between colleagues. This simple self-monitoring tool can help us learn about ourselves as well as others. In fact, when working cross-culturally, we learn a lot more about ourselves than about anyone else! When working mono-culturally, which is pretty much impossible today, our assumptions about the "right" way to do things are never challenged. Just ask a fish how he feels about the water. Only when a norm has been changed—when the fish is removed from the water—is it noted.

Saphiere

I had a very unfortunate experience with a client a few months ago. There was a Nigerian project manager working in Belgium who had been there for about a year. He called a meeting that was attended by the three Europe-based engineers he had invited. These four guys in the meeting room greet each other in English and start out talking in English, and just as the Nigerian manager is about to introduce the task at hand, the local engineers start talking about the project very excitedly in French. They go on and on and they're quite animated and enthusiastic about the project. Forty-five minutes later, all four of the men stand up and shake hands, and a Belgian says in English, "Well, I think this solution will work very well."

The Nigerian looks at him with a very disgusted face and says, "What solution?"

The Belgian looks at him and asks, "Do you not speak French? Didn't you understand what we said?"

He said, "Of course I don't speak French! I'm the manager here; why did you switch into French? You didn't ask me; why didn't you talk to me in English?" They were totally passing each other like ships in the night.

We look at an incident like that, and we wonder, "Who's right?" Do they need to speak French? Do they need to speak English? The Nigerian manager thought they should have respected his leadership by asking him or following his lead. These four men had different expectations about leadership and meetings, and on top of that, there was a history of oppression that got in the way. The problem was in the assumptions and stereotypes.

That's basically what Kathleen and I deal with. At the fundamental level, we feel there are three basic cross-cultural capacities. The first one is knowing ourselves—knowing ourselves as cultural beings, how we have learned to approach life and to make decisions, recognizing that the way that we have of doing things is only one way out of a lot of options. Our way is not "the" right way. Subjective culture means being able to understand our own expectations so that we can anticipate them and explain them better to other people. So the first competence is subjective culture—knowing yourself.

The second is what we call cultural literacy, which basically sounds like the ability to read another person. It starts with giving somebody else the benefit of the doubt rather than jumping to conclusions that are too often negative. It's taking a step back when somebody is doing something that appears to be incompetent or rude and thinking for a second, "What could be the positive intent behind this? What could this person be trying achieve that I might be unaware of because of how I've been brought up to approach a problem?"

So then the third step really is, "Okay, I see how I want to do things, and I see how this person wants to do things, now let's bridge these cultures so that we use the assets I'm bringing to the table and we also use the assets and abilities that this other person is contributing." Those cultural bridges involve interpersonal skills, and they also require structures and systems on an organizational or community level that will support those interpersonal skills.

Curran

The third step—the building of bridges and finding a balance among differences—is just not something that we naturally do, especially when we have a job to do and a deadline to meet. Yet it's probably the most significant part of intercultural competence. We can identify and recognize differences in our approaches and motivating values; but real competence is being able to *do* something with the knowledge. Imagine the essentials of an actual bridge: connecting two points, designed well so that it can withstand the elements, appropriate for the need and environment, constructed of sound materials—all the fundamental features of the actual bridge provide the same support for an effective cultural bridge.

Wright

People in organizations seem very fast-paced and deadline-driven. What are some of the most common pitfalls you have seen in this global work environment?

Curran

I think the time crunch is, in fact, one barrier many often see as an obstacle to growing their global skills "We don't have time to devote effort to developing intercultural competence!" Therefore, they're so prone to falling into common pitfalls.

In our experience, a few pitfalls readily come to mind. The first one is related to time: going too fast in terms of language use and our pace of speaking, as well as in terms of our knowledge and experience, and the expectations that go with that. For example, sometimes in the United States, we may talk over each other a bit because we know that one is ending his or her sentence or point, and we grab the chance to take the floor. We prefer a good quick pace to our conversations because this can show engagement and presence. People trying to get a word in may have difficulties if they don't follow those same "rules." In contrast, members of Asian cultures, generally speaking, often wait for one to finish before the next person begins to speak. This shows respect to both the speaker and the point being made. So when an Asian can finally provide his or her input, it might be on something that's already been discussed. Many times in multicultural groups, I've heard an exasperated exclamation when someone raises a question or adds a comment that is on a topic that has passed: "Why didn't you tell us that sooner?" He or she probably tried, but couldn't get the floor. That lack of awareness about differing uses of a common language is a very common pitfall.

The same pitfall, going too fast, happens when the depth of knowledge and experience with a subject among team members varies. If, for example, I have been with a project for quite a number of years, I have a greater depth of understanding and will probably execute more quickly. I don't need to spend time gaining more context or looking for greater breadth or depth of information. But another, not having that same amount of history or experience, may not be able to run with the project quite as quickly. Another factor to consider around going too fast is in terms of problem-solving styles. Maybe I just want the big picture—the treetops in three bullets—while another might need the whole tree in order to know the conclusion as well as the background of how that conclusion was reached before being able to solve a problem. I've seen this pitfall occur very often, especially in global virtual teams. Generally, at headquarters or a main site, most have a significant amount of knowledge about a project, while people in the subsidiary have less, so there can be a mismatch in pace, knowledge, expectations, and problem-solving approaches.

The next problem then is relying on assumptions. It's related because we very often assume understanding, similar to Dianne's previous example of the Nigerian project manager—assuming understanding, assuming we're both on the same page. There's a tendency to over-estimate the leveling effects of organizational culture. We assume because we all work for X, Y, or Z organization, that we share the same approaches, processes, and language. In fact, one interesting question I heard recently was, "Because we're so global and we have the same processes, does culture really matter?" The answer is clearly "yes!"

A great amount of assuming understanding occurs because we may be using the same language. The most common language of business today is English. So when many organizations use English as the shared language, it may be very easy to hear accent differences but very easy to forget that the way we use the language may differ greatly.

Again, I can give an example from my experience in Malaysia. Leaving a restaurant, my Malaysian colleague told her counterpart from Australia, "Les, I'll follow you back." Does this phrase, "follow you back" mean going together in the same car or behind in a separate one? When Les from Australia heard this phrase, she got in her car and drove off, leaving her Malaysian colleague standing in dismay on the curb! In Malaysia, "follow you back" means going together in the same car. A very significant difference in the interpretation of those simple words!

If we assume understanding because of using a common language, you can imagine how idioms in English can present another pitfall. Idioms are colorful and clear to one who's familiar with them, but often a mystery to another. One team member in the United States attempted to spur her Chinese colleagues on by saying, "Hurry up team; I'm behind the rabbit!" How might that translate? Her Chinese colleague may understand the meaning of every word, but the meaning of the expression? Probably not. Over-estimating the similarities of a common organizational culture and organizational language is a pitfall many fall into.

The last pitfall I've often seen is one coming to a task thinking, "my way is the best way," which often occurs because we have a job to do and we are pressured by a deadline. This looks like: "Let me show you. I have a solution. This is how to do it." These kinds of statements are made without learning what the other person does already, what works already. Such a bulldozing "my way is the best way" attitude can come across as arrogant and ethnocentric. If there's any cultural luggage (not baggage) one should carry when working globally, it is an attitude of learning—the desire to discover another's perspective and another's approach. Nothing shows respect like listening to and seeing another's point of view—perhaps not agreeing with it, but at least demonstrating a desire to learn about another's approach or process.

Wright

What are some of the most common mistakes you see people making when they work cross-culturally or live in a multicultural community?

Curran

These are very much related to the pitfalls. The first is forgetting to check out our interpretation—not taking off our own glasses—thereby using our own cultural rules or seeing through our own cultural lens. For example, at a team meeting in Indonesia, a team leader from the United States was really frustrated with the lack of participation at the table. I'm not sure if you've experienced this in your meetings, David, but this team had a leader who was trying to get peoples' opinions and ideas verbally and spontaneously. It was a typical brainstorming session. When few participated, he was quite frustrated and even critical of his team. In his eyes, no participation equaled no interest and no ideas. He concluded his team had no initiative. Yet the team members were actually showing respect for him in the role of a leader by not challenging him! They were showing group cohesiveness by not contradicting each other. These were very appropriate behaviors in the Indonesian culture, but practically opposite to expectations in the North American culture. This negative perception occurred because that team leader hadn't removed his own cultural lens and checked out the influence of his interpretation on his Indonesian team members' behaviors.

I think another common mistake that I've often seen (and have been guilty of myself) is not practicing communication style flexibility. Here's another story. A Singaporean colleague of mine was scheduled to make a presentation at a special closed meeting, but since the topic was interesting to me, I asked her directly, "May I attend?" I expected a simple yes or no answer.

She hesitated, "Oh, you know, the other presenters may feel uncomfortable if a stranger is sitting in the audience."

I responded to what I perceived as an excuse with an assurance that I would stay out of sight. I felt I had logically countered her reason and she'd say okay, but then she said, "Well, the participants may feel awkward if you are there, and you may feel frustrated because you can't participate."

And to both of those I again said, "Oh, not to worry, I will stay out of the way."

Finally, she loudly and quite heatedly said, "No, you can't come!"

I was shocked at what I perceived to be a very unprofessional overreaction. Why didn't she just say no? Of course she had been indirectly screaming "no!" I just didn't get it. I hadn't flexed my communication style to understand her way of telling me; I was just listening for what I wanted to hear. And again, there were repercussions from this conversation. Our subsequent relationship was clearly strained and our ability to work together negatively affected.

These examples show that intercultural competence is like gaining fluency in a language. When fluent, we have command over the language and can select the word, phrase, grammatical structure, and tone of voice to best suit the person we are interacting with, the purpose of the interaction, and the context in which we are interacting, for example, a cocktail party with friends or a business negotiation with a new client. In each, we may choose different topics, different words, different tones, and so on. It is the mindful and strategic flexibility that equals competence in intercultural communication.

What doesn't work for working across cultures? We don't recommend following a list of do's and don'ts of what will not offend, such as "don't show the sole of your shoe in the Middle East," or "don't make eye contact in Japan." If we provide ten do's and don'ts, you will inevitably run into number eleven. Such protocol is important, but such an approach is limited. And with the dynamism of cultures, you may find your do's and don'ts become outdated or situationally inappropriate quite quickly.

Other cross-cultural approaches that don't work are those that say "Bulgarians are hierarchical" or "Germans are direct." Generalizations can be valuable places to start, but there is a great diversity of people in every culture, and so much depends on the context of the situation and the definition of the terminology.

Wright

So how do you help individuals and organizations find success in this fast-paced global environment? As you've been working in the international, intercultural business interface for nearly fifty years combined, would you tell us about one or two of your favorite projects and what success looks like?

Saphiere

I'm happy to, David. My all-time favorite project was work I did over a period of about ten years with a specialty chemical company. The best practice for them was that they approached intercultural effectiveness from an organizational and systemic level. As a cross-cultural consultant, I was able to participate in their executive staff meetings and conduct periodic learning sessions during those meetings. Intercultural was also an aspect of every merger and acquisition in which they engaged.

The favorite part of my job though was much more practical. I'm a very hands-on person, and when I worked for this company in its Japan operation, everybody who traveled into Japan from overseas had a "meet with Dianne" conversation at the beginning of his or her trip. It was wonderful because before people arrived, I was able to meet with the local Japanese staff that they'd work with to understand the business issues and what the Japanese customers wanted, what the offices in Osaka or Fukuoka wanted, and I was able to coach the Japanese a little bit on how to work with the international visitor. So then when people from France or from the United States came into Tokyo, I could meet with them and say, "What are you trying to achieve from this business trip? What are your objectives? What's your strategy?" Then the main part of our discussion was to determine, "If this is your objective, you probably want to modify your strategy a little bit this way—try presenting it to your counterparts here in Japan in this manner." Then we were able to pull in the Japanese counterparts as well and do a little bit of team building at the very start of that business trip. So it got them off on such a great footing. It was two-way, and it was task-focused on exactly the business they were doing at the time.

The results were that this Japan operation was the first overseas organization in the entire corporation to have a local president; that came as a result of these efforts. Up until this point, the organization had their scientists in Japan, their scientists in Europe, and the ones in the United States. They began cross-pollinating and sending scientists for long-term assignments across the oceans. It became a much more global company in which they started making decisions together and planning: "Okay, the Japanese are good at this and we're good at this, so how can we coordinate it?" So that would be one example from my experience.

Curran

The management and executive team level is another in which we often work, which really is a success strategy right there. Having upper level support sends a clear message throughout the whole organization as to the importance of intercultural effectiveness. One of my favorite team-level interventions was with a very large power company that was trying to incorporate intercultural skills into every strategic management meeting. At every management meeting held in a different part of the world, we integrated modules of cross-cultural training and focused strategic practice elements. They looked at their own task-specific challenges, then explored possible cultural influences that may have been preventing things from working as smoothly as they'd like. Together, inclusively, they tried to find solutions that worked for everyone.

We've been putting a lot of work into recognizing, understanding, and tapping the cultural differences at two levels: 1) Cross border: French, Brazilian, Swiss, Canadian, Indian, Chinese, British, Spanish, Norwegian, and 2) Cross-functional at the business unit level—the manufacturing and engineering groups. They have, in fact, found they have been removing the "personal" and realizing the "cultural." In other words, a difference is now not seen as one's "odd way of working"—they realized it's a culturally influenced approach. There have been so many "ah-ha's" that it's been really rewarding, especially in areas such as leading changes, transferring knowledge, presenting or persuading others, and changing the way they package their information, resulting in enhanced credibility and acceptance. They have incorporated such questions into daily practice: What does what I'm trying to do look like in different cultures? What might the recipient or listener look for and expect? How can I adapt my message or approach or argument for a better connection?

So they are working on producing a global team charter which enables them to develop their vision in such a way that it really respects and includes all and clarifies who's to do what, how operations and procedures will work, and what communication processes will be used to connect the team. I think that the results are really impressive because they're at the individual as well at the systemic levels. They've reported increased cross-cultural understanding, feeling a greater sense of community and very importantly, greater trust, stronger communication channels, definite evidence of aligning their manufacturing and engineering business units so they have streamlined processes that are going to be, in the end, very financially rewarding. All of their work has really done a lot to raise the idea of cultural differences to a level that people can discuss. Cross-cultural differences are now a usable platform, so now the awareness has more validity and their intercultural effectiveness skills help to support the integration and streamlining of their processes.

Another favorite project I want to mention is one that targets the individual level. I'm working with a global leadership development program in Asia using the intercultural competency process as a tool for helping executives lead by influence, not authority. This challenge is a common phenomenon today with global teams. Very often, a global team leader must lead a cross-border, cross-functional, cross-business unit team without having resource control. While a major source of stress, this can also be a major source of opportunity—if one can capitalize on the diversity. The approach suggests that when the team leader can connect the project vision to the cultural context and the needs of each member and show understanding of the cultural norms and practices of each team member, team members will want to prioritize that project. Team leaders are taking action to cultivate a very open and productive climate that is balanced, as opposed to one that is overly task focused and neglects the "people part." It's a way of connecting with the heart, not just the head or the hands. While we don't have tangible results yet, participants resonate with the approach. This looks like intercultural effectiveness skills may significantly contribute to the success of those leading by influence, not authority.

Lastly, we also work with expatriates who are relocating to a new culture to accomplish specific corporate objectives. These clients consistently report that developing intercultural skills before going on their assignment enables them to better manage expectations, gain insights that help them understand the cultural differences they encounter, and not make as many mistakes that could have impacted their business success! Such outcomes are incredibly significant, though not always clearly measurable by dollars and cents.

Saphiere

Yes, all of our favorite projects obviously are ones in which our clients reap the benefits of cultural differences and are able to make major business improvements.

You know, like any consultant, we enjoy it when we feel like our work really makes a difference.

So to summarize, I think there are two key success factors. One is that the clients adjust their formula for measuring success so that it includes intercultural effectiveness. Whether they use Balanced Score Card or any other metrics they see as critical, it has to include a look at how interculturally competent they are, and whether they are developing that competency in their management and in the organization.

The second success factor is recognizing the need to balance global consistency and a strong corporate culture with local appropriateness. Too often companies think globalization is about standardization. They come to us for the answer. But the answer isn't *what* to do, it's *how*—a focus on process improvement, an ongoing process of engagement and balancing that enables us to hear the diverse perspectives, understand them, and create together new ways of working that harness the differences. In this manner, differences lead to cost savings, error reductions, enhanced productivity, and job satisfaction.

Wright

The theme of this book is "success strategies." What are some of the most important personal strategies for intercultural success?

Saphiere

I like that you asked us about the personal strategies because intercultural effectiveness really does start with each one of us. We're like pebbles dropped into a pond—the point of contact creates the ripples although the power is in the critical mass. Let me share one more story with you. There was a very high-ranking U.S. American executive in a class that I was teaching. She was working with a group of Dutch IT professionals. She raised her hand and basically announced to the class, "The Dutch are sexist, they lack a work ethic, and I'm amazed that they are able to stay competitive in the world market because they don't work that hard." Pretty much the whole class had their mouths hanging open as they heard this high-ranking woman declare this. We've all heard a lot of biases in our day, but this was a new one. What had led to such harsh judgments?

This woman ran a business unit and her internal IT support—the people who provided the business and the technical support her unit needed to be successful—

was based in the Netherlands. She had a huge new project come up and she had e-mailed her IT people and had asked them to develop a new software system for her unit. The Dutch guys e-mailed her back and said quite clearly, "No, we can't do that for you. Our projects have already been booked for the rest of the year." Well, she was put off by this very direct and negative answer; she felt it rude and lacking in a service orientation. She wrote back to them, "You are my internal IT support. It's your job to help us with this. If we're going to make our sales projections for the year, we're dependent on you and we need this new system. We, of course, will pay you for your time and cover the costs, but please let me know when the project can begin."

So again, there was this total crosstalk. As she was talking about it to us in the class, she said, "So these Dutch guys write back to me, and to add to their initial negativity, they then said that England and Germany had huge projects coming up and they had priority over what we are doing in the United States! So not only did they not respect me because I'm a woman, but they're Euro-centric as well!" She made these poor guys sound like such villains.

Probably most of us hear a story like this and we think, "Oh, I wouldn't react that way." But I've been doing this work for twenty-seven years. I know that when push comes to shove, we *all* react this way in some situation or another; it's just what happens to push our buttons. In this situation this woman was so convinced that she was correct in her beliefs that it took us two days during class to convince her to try to see if she could give them the benefit of the doubt. We tried to help her see that their directness was motivated out of respect for her. They weren't valuing diplomacy as she was; they were valuing honesty. They didn't want to mislead her and waste her time, and indeed their schedules had already been set for the year. Their IT department was very process-oriented and they scheduled a year ahead. Many of us here in the States think we're direct and we want to be honest, but as this story illustrates, we also like verbal softeners and a little bit of diplomacy. She was a senior executive and "how dare" they talk to her without any of those softeners! It was a matter of style and values. On her part, she had an American "can do" mentality: "Hey, it's important and we have to work as hard as we need to do to get it done!" You know, NIKE, "Let's Do It!" But in the Dutch sense, they valued work/life balance and they are probably a lot better at it than the average U.S. American.

So in this case, she ended up going over to Amsterdam to meet with the IT guys. She asked questions about how they approach IT and how they do their yearly planning. She listened to them, and she listened enough that they backed off a little bit and thought to themselves, "Okay, maybe this witchy, arrogant woman isn't quite so evil after all; maybe it's a miscommunication." It ended up being good for everybody, because she was able to get them to build some flexibility into their planning system so they could respond to emerging market needs. She in turn learned a little bit about planning ahead and trying to coordinate. It points out to me that we're all born ethnocentric. We're all born thinking "our way is the right way"—ethno-relativism is really a learned competency.

Curran

You asked about the key personal success strategy, David. From Dianne's story, we can see several of the most important personal strategies that we can all practice immediately. The first is that attitude of curiosity and learning. As I've said before, nothing shows greater respect and opens the channels of communication better than wanting to discover and learn about somebody else's way of seeing things.

Another is listening to learn, not just to convince or to overpower and prove your point. It's a totally different way of listening; it's more open and conveys the message, "Let me hear your stories and learn about your point of view."

A third success strategy is taking moments of reflection to ask, how will what I do or say be perceived? This split second of empathy before you open your mouth or before you pick up the phone or click send on the computer can help prevent many, many unintentional misunderstandings and miscommunication.

Another personal success strategy is looking for the positive intent as a new way of framing what we see and what we experience. We all do what we do because we believe it's the best way—the best way to communicate, to solve our problems, to make a decision, to use our time, or whatever. We don't do most things because we think they are wrong. So looking for the positive intent creates the climate—the openness and the potential for building those strong and productive bridges.

And the last personal success strategy everyone can practice is seeking the "both-and," not the "either-or." In fact, presenting only polar options is actually a fallacy in reasoning, and not realistic. Either-or frames set up defenses, too—a desire to be "right or wrong," to do it "your way or my way." So a personal success strategy is shifting that mindset or re-framing so you look to find what is valuable in all perspectives, and create from there. You've actually then just created more resources out of what looked like opposition. And you notice too that these personal success strategies involve the three capacities we mentioned: subjective culture (or knowing yourself), cultural literacy (or learning about others), and cultural bridging.

Wright

What about organizational success strategies? So many organizations today are multicultural or international.

Curran

They *all* are actually—even yours. Basically what we are saying is that in addition to building greater awareness of the impact of cultural differences on our personal communication, look at the bigger picture across the organization. What systems support and continue cultural learning and intercultural effectiveness?

Saphiere

Yes, on the strategic level I talked a little bit about the semiconductor company that I had worked with that was trying to combine four different divisions into one. We ended up working with them for about nine months on this because they were trying to combine the manufacturing, sales, research, and engineering organizations. Three of the four directors had come in deciding ahead of time that, "We're going to do away with the research guy. Research is pie-in-the-sky, blue sky, green fields anyway; they don't bring in quick income. We'll cut and slash that whole division and save the multi-million dollars that we need."

By the end of the nine months, they actually ended up putting that head of the research division in charge of the new combined division, so it was a complete turnaround. They ended up saving almost a hundred million dollars in that first year, and they didn't lay off any people. So even though it might not be the classical way that we think of "culture" in the international sense, it was definitely the cross-cultural approach that enabled them to streamline the organization and combine the four different divisions.

Curran

Another example at this strategic level is, again, from our earlier conversation about the logistics company with the promotion-from-within policy that few Southeast

Asians were taking advantage of. The question was, is there a cultural reason behind the meager uptake? The answer was yes. The fundamentals of that policy were very United States culture driven; seeking a promotion was up to the individual's initiative. After seeing a potential job posted, it would be up to that individual to go for it, assess his or her own skills and potential, enlist the manager's support, and individually drive that process. This is not the norm in many local organizations in Southeast Asia; so for starters, the process for posting openings had not been implemented culturally appropriately. Posting job openings in the cafeteria was too public, too open to possible loss of face for applicants who tried but were not successful.

Most significantly, in the course of interviewing employees at this organization, I found very different assumptions and expectations regarding who should take the initiative and drive the career development process. U.S. managers were waiting for the local employees to attempt the promotion process, and the local employees were waiting for the U.S. managers to point out to the employee that she or he had the skills that would make them appropriate for applying for the promotion. So each was waiting for the other—appropriate behavior to each one's cultural norms, I might add. We worked with the internal industrial psychologist to develop a competency based assessment system. Individuals were supported in becoming better able to assess in a behavioral manner what their skills were and what needed to be developed. A more private method for announcing those promotion opportunities was implemented, and we then created a tool for opening the promotion opportunity conversation between the manager and the employees. All in all, the process then had much less inherent risk for anyone to lose face at any point. These systemic strategic changes really shifted the implementation of this policy, and now the management pool has plenty of possibilities.

Saphiere

So the question was what are key organizational success strategies for intercultural success? As we can see from these examples, communication and effort must be two-way. Organizations need to develop a critical mass for changes to happen; you can't have just one person responsible. We need structures that support intercultural competence, like hiring systems in which the criteria for selection is based on job competence. If English fluency is not a job requirement, don't interview in English. If local management must play a key role in selection, review criteria for cultural bias so that selection committees understand what "leadership" looks like in Warsaw versus in Chicago. Promotion systems and corporate cultures must also be attended to—are you hiring diversity only to squeeze it out by forcing people to fit in with an overly narrow and limiting definition of "corporate"?

Wright

A big part of success is using the right tool or resource. Would you share with us a few of your favorites that readers could use to improve their own intercultural success?

Curran

Dianne is the queen of tools, while I'm focused more on facilitation, coaching, and consulting. The most significant tool that we are both very involved with is called *Cultural Detective*®. It's a tool that builds on the metaphor of being a detective—seeking clues to understand what is going on. So if you imagine a magnifying glass as a cultural lens through which the world is viewed, how would it look? What we expect, our values, our common sense, what we see, how we see it and how we respond—that's our lens on the world.

Saphiere

Yes, the *Cultural Detective*® is a collaborative project. There are about one hundred of the best organizational psychologists, sociologists, anthropologists, interculturalists, and management experts in the world working on it. It's based upon a core methodology that is theoretically sound and enables deep understanding and effectiveness very quickly. The wonderful thing about the *Cultural Detective*® is that it helps people at different geographic locations within an organization, as well as different functional locations, to develop a common vocabulary and a shared mindset around effectiveness; then they can use that core method to resolve conflict as it occurs. They can use it to create solutions that work in complex environments. They use it to reflect on and learn from their individual as well as their team experience. And they can use it to plan project rollouts in a culturally astute manner.

The *Cultural Detective*® helps you understand your own lens and how you view the world. You're then able to contrast that with at least forty other cultural lenses, so you can compare and contrast the similarities and the differences that you might have with some of your team members. And then you can build those bridges that we were talking about.

The detective metaphor has proved to be very powerful for developing intercultural competence—understanding our own cultural drivers, insight to another's, and the skills and systems to bridge the differences and leverage similarities for productive results.

Curran

Other tools that are very powerful for us are those that are experiential. Most of our clients are adult learners who learn best via activities that relate directly to their realities and needs, and draw on their personal experiences.

Other resources we go to include Dianne's co-authored work, *Communication Highwire*; Charles Hampden-Turner's *Dilemma Reconciliation*; Barry Johnson's *Polarity Management*; Appreciative Inquiry; Bennett's *Developmental Model of Intercultural Sensitivity*; and Stella Ting-Toomey's Conflict and Face Negotiation work.

Wright

What is your vision for individuals and organizations that adopt and implement your success strategies, and develop their intercultural effectiveness?

Saphiere

My key vision is that our clients develop a sustainable competitive advantage, not just over the short-term, but real long-term growth and success because they are harnessing the assets of the diversity of every global team member throughout their workforce and the communities they impact. So, my vision is that organizations truly view and use differences as assets.

Curran

Another vision that I feel strongly about is building the truly global organization, which is much more than being geographically dispersed, more than gaining revenues from worldwide locations, or having employees around the world. Rather, in a truly global organization, from the individual to the team to leadership, the intercultural perspective is supported and integrated into key strategy, systems, and solutions.

Saphiere

Leaders at every level will have the global mindset that enables them to see the validity and the value in a broad range of approaches that can seem contradictory. Intercultural skills help you explore and balance those apparent contradictions—those different pulls and priorities and preferences and perspectives—to create innovative solutions that are the best of both rather than a choice between existing solutions, and create a new solution that harnesses the contributions of all stakeholders.

Curran

Today too, as I'm sure you and our readers are aware, one of the biggest challenges many organizations face is how to attract and retain the best talent. Whether due to the aging of the population, or in some cases, a shortage of key skills and talents, many organizations cite this as one of their biggest concerns. We believe that organizations that implement these kinds of strategies for developing intercultural effectiveness can become preferred places to work.

Such organizations work to cultivate an environment in which different perspectives are viewed as positive creative input and where new ideas are valued and not seen as "rocking the boat." Much literature suggests that this kind of open climate and fertile environment attracts the best talent from around the globe and contributes to people wanting to stay and work for you.

In *The Flight of the Creative Class,* Richard Florida states that global competition needs the three T's: Technology, Talent, and most importantly, Tolerance. Tolerance to us means openness and a positive approach toward diversity, a creative environment that provides the capacity to grow. And when an environment is proactively inclusive, employees stay and the organization has the advantage of harnessing their creative capabilities. So that's a really timely and practical application of the advantages of developing intercultural effectiveness.

Wright

Since intercultural communication is such a vital need for everyone in today's dynamic global business environment, what is a key take-away message for every reader?

Curran

We've crystallized this message for our readers down to one simple phrase that everyone can apply immediately: "The attitude of discovery—don't leave home without it!"

Wright

This has been a great conversation, and I have learned a lot here today about things I have never even thought about before. You've set me on a new path, and I'm sure that our readers will gain a lot from this chapter.

I really appreciate all the time that both of you have taken here today to answer all these questions!

Curran

Thank you very much for your time as well, David.

Saphiere

It's been a pleasure.

About Dianne Hofner Saphiere & Kathleen Curran

Dianne founded Nipporica Associates LLC, an intercultural management-consulting firm, in 1989 after working a decade with a larger consulting group. She is the creator of the highly acclaimed *Cultural Detective*® series, and founder and co-moderator of the online knowledge-sharing platform for interculturalists worldwide, *Intercultural Insights*. Dianne is blessed with a terrific husband and son.

Her authored works include *Ecotonos: A Simulation on Multicultural Collaboration,* now in its fifth printing with Intercultural Press; *Redundancía: A Foreign Language Simulation*; and an audio CD and manual, *Shinrai: Building Trusting Relationships with Japanese Colleagues*. Dianne co-authored *Communication Highwire: Leveraging the Power of Diverse Communication Styles* with Barbara Kappler Mikk and Basma Ibrahim DeVries, published by Intercultural Press in 2005. She is also a frequent contributor to edited volumes.

Dianne holds an MS in Human Resources and Organizational Development, a BA in International Studies, as well as extensive post-graduate professional development certifications.

Kathleen is the founder and principal consultant of Intercultural Systems, a global intercultural consulting, coaching, and training firm founded in Singapore in 1996, with offices in both Singapore and Houston, Texas. She has lived and worked in Asia for over twenty years. Spanning three continents and cyberspace, her global work in leadership development, strategic cross-cultural change management, and multicultural teambuilding has served clients in government agencies, educational institutions, and Global 500 corporations in the hydropower, media, oil and gas, aerospace, banking, bio/pharmaceutical, electronics, and logistics sectors.

Kathleen holds an MA in Intercultural Communication and a BA in Linguistics from the University of Texas at Austin and is a graduate of Corporate Coach University. She has held faculty positions with Institut Teknologi Mara (Malaysia), the University of Maryland's European and Asian Divisions, Ngee Ann Polytechnic (Singapore), and the Royal Melbourne Institute of Technology, Singapore campus, and served as advisor/liaison to the Saudi Arabian Ministry of Foreign Affairs and King Saud University. She is co-author of *Cultural Detective®: Singapore* and *Cultural Detective®: Malaysia* and a frequent speaker on current challenges and choices in the global workplace, especially pertaining to Southeast Asian cultures and women working globally.

Dianne Hofner Saphiere
Nipporica Associates
N 1108, 2028 Avenida del Mar
Fracc. Telleŕias
82140 Mazatlán, Sinaloa México
+1-913-901-0243
dianne@culturaldetective.com
www.CulturalDetective.com

Kathleen A. Curran
Intercultural Systems
516 South Post Oak Lane #6
Houston, TX 77056 USA
+1 (713) 305-8258 / +65 9758-8483
Kathleen@intercultural-systems.com
www.intercultural-systems.com